Diary of Agony and Hope

Diary of Agony and Hope

Waves of Folk Sayings in the Ferguson Movement

What's really behind
Funky Rhythms and
Deep Cries of the
Ferguson Movement?

E. HAMMOND OGLESBY

RESOURCE *Publications* • Eugene, Oregon

DIARY OF AGONY AND HOPE
Waves of Folk Sayings in the Ferguson Movement

Copyright © 2015 E. Hammond Oglesby. All rights reserved. Except for brief quotations in critical publications or reviews, no part of this book may be reproduced in any manner without prior written permission from the publisher. Write: Permissions, Wipf and Stock Publishers, 199 W. 8th Ave., Suite 3, Eugene, OR 97401.

Resource Publications
An Imprint of Wipf and Stock Publishers
199 W. 8th Ave., Suite 3
Eugene, OR 97401

www.wipfandstock.com

ISBN 13: 978-1-4982-3168-8

Manufactured in the U.S.A.   10/26/2015

Dedicated to:
Rev. Enoch Hammond, my grandpa
and
Ashton Jacob Oglesby, my grandson

Grandson, Ashton Oglesby, held by President-Elect, Barack Obama, 2007, Detroit, MI.

Contents

Acknowledgments | ix
Preface | xi

1 Ferguson: A Historical Look | 1
2 Waves and Voices from the Otherside | 5
3 Waves of White Anger vs. Black Response | 13
4 Waves of Lament and Hope | 30
5 Case Studies | 48
6 Study Questions | 61

Bibliography | 65
About the Author | 67

Acknowledgments

I gave my energy to these observations and reflections, in this small volume, *Diary of Agony and Hope,* not because I am anyone in particular – as a resident of St. Louis – but because I care deeply about the American value of social justice. For example, the moral dictum which has guided my inward passion – in the rhythmic, and at times painful journey of this diary – is anchored in the words of Holy Scripture: "He has told you, O mortal, what is good; and what does the Lord require of you but to do justice, and to love kindness, and to walk humbly with your God?" (Micah 6:8).

Firstly, it was about the gradual knowledge about the amazing history of the city of Ferguson that caught me by surprise as a writer. From a historical perspective, I find many of its customary symbols and cultural icons simply fascinating – especially the functional role of the "train whistle" in the regulative order of daily life in Ferguson. *Secondly*, this book of mine is a gift as much as it is an agonizing labor of ethical discourse, because I have walked the same streets where urban unrest took place. I have shopped in supermarkets and other stores along the main avenues of Ferguson where violence and burnings took place. History being partial to irony and surprise, I have also enjoyed fine food and entertainment among ordinary folk, who often say: "We Love Ferguson!"

I would like to acknowledge the extraordinary debt I owe to Margret O. Sidney, who spent tireless hours in preparation of this manuscript. I want to mention a special person, Gloria P. Oglesby, my wife, who gave me continual support, helpful suggestions, and love.

Preface

This little diary is all about a big agonizing hunger in the heartland of American Life: the hunger for healing, the hunger for reconciliation, the hunger for justice, and the hunger for <u>transformation</u> and progress in the face of brokenness and mistrust between police officers and young black teens in particular – to say the least. The Bible gives witness in the following matter: *"Evening, and morning, and at noon, will I pray and cry aloud: and God shall hear my voice"* (Ps 55:17). Well, the voices of the Ferguson movement have thundered in high and low places in our Democratic Republic and from around the world.

    Even our Commander-in-Chief, President Barack Obama has taken notice, and appears to express deep moral concern in regard to patterns of unrest in the city of Ferguson and elsewhere in our nation. As I recall, pieces of this diary actually began to emerge a long time ago, when Barack Obama was running as a presidential candidate. Born in Hawaii to a mother from Kansas and a father from Kenya, Mr. Obama – to the amazement of countless millions of ordinary people – became our forty-fourth president of the United States of America, in 2008. He himself became the first black man to occupy the highest political office in the land as Commander-in Chief. What an astonishing achievement that still gives hope to ordinary folk, who will not accept adversity or present location, as a way to determine one's destination. Of course, racial disturbances in Ferguson caught everybody – seemingly – by surprise. Raw emotions by some protestors, in my opinion, do not overshadow the racial and ethnic progress already made –politically, socially, and economically. For example, in an unexpected photo cited earlier, but uniquely surprising, one of my little grandsons was affectionately held at a political rally in Detroit, Michigan, and held by then, Presidential Candidate Obama.

Who can really estimate – concretely and symbolically the historic significance of America's move to elect its first black Commander-in-Chief, President Barack Obama? What tears of joy, hope, and promise did many American citizens shed, in 2008! For many tearful eyes of promise, signaled the dawn of a new day had suddenly begun. For many of us, the bitter pill of disbelief laced in the historical drama of racial bigotry – which was overshadowed with the joyful belief, "Yes We Can," Yes, We Have!

What a life-changing and precious moment for me in time – as a person of color, as an obscure community organizer from Chicago, had been immersed, apparently, and captivated by the impossible possibility of moving, as it were, from the "Outhouse" to the "White House." In the rhythmic flux of time and space, many writers and journalists will examine and celebrate the milestone of Barack Obama as the first black man to serve as President of the United States of America. Beyond, the mere raw emotions and words, something deep in my heart and soul changed. Something different about me had changed. Something about my fellow Americans had changed, about my white brothers and sisters – who marched – when duty called – to the beat of the Red, White and Blue flag – in the security of our nation or in the cause of Freedom, Justice and human rights around the world.

Yet, these noble vibes so common to many Americans of goodwill do not eliminate the pain and hurt around the hearts of many protestors for Michael Brown, his family, and the voices that cry out for change. While progress has and is being made; we are not there yet. To be sure, voices from the other side must be reckoned with.

Contextually, I am an ordained minister of the gospel of Jesus Christ; I am a retired professor of social ethics and theology, who served at Eden Theological Seminary for nearly 30 years. At that

Preface

time, I was the first full-time African American on the faculty in the 128 year history of the school. I am a proud Missourian, who received an honorable "Resolution" citation from the Missouri House of Representatives. In language peculiar to elected public officials, the formal resolution reflected eight literary expressions of "Whereas" – beginning with the following: "Whereas, the members of the Missouri House of Representatives hold in high esteem those Show-Me State residents who have proven down through the years to be exemplar citizens in local communities . . . through the excellence of their spiritual and educational leadership . . .. Now, therefore be it resolved that we . . . convey to him best wishes."
Missouri House Resolution, 2587, adopted May 5, 2008

I am a resident of St. Louis County for over three decades. Be that as it may, I am also a little league soccer coach and baseball fan. We affectionately call St. Louis home. As certain folk told us upon arrival in St. Louis many years ago, "take it from me, man; St. Louis can be a fine city to raise your family. We got the best Zoo in the world for young children to hang-out . . . and it's free!" Checkout those World Series Red Birds! Yes, we got the Gateway Arch overlooking the mighty Mississippi River. Tasty food from all ethnic groups, including Sweetie Pie, Upper Crust; Celebrity Soul Food —- just to name a few."

For ordinary folk, these expressions say a lot about St. Louis itself. Its wave of civic pride pierced the air – like the wings of a red bird flying above our multicultural landscape. And the rhythmic beat goes on and on in regard to our medical and religious centers that showcase – impart – our common life, banked against the shadows of the mighty Mississippi River. Suddenly, out of nowhere – seemingly – came the thundering noise, shocked and painfully surprised, of Ferguson. The tragic shooting of Michael Brown, Jr. by police office Darren Wilson, on August 9, 2014, triggered a wave of protest – ending in deep hurt, violence, rage, burnings, and the loss of property.

Undoubtedly, it is the burden of race we live with everyday. For example, my wife and I are blessed with two sons. They are African Americans. As parents, we went the second mile to teach them the values of respect for police officers, patriotic loyalty, hard work, and educational excellence in the community.

As a resident of St. Louis County, I conveyed to them my caution about being extremely respectful to police officers while away from home – i.e., some may kill you with the blick-of-an-eye, unfortunately or mistakenly, because of the color of your skin! As a responsible father, this dreadful fear, apparently, or mistrust of cops did not grow out of disrespect for the hard job they do on a daily basis to secure our safety and to protect the common good.

Rather this dreadful feeling – sometimes – in the pit of my stomach grew out of, it seems, the basic impulse for survival of young black teens living in contemporary American society. Atlas, I don't think that I am alone in this ethical burden of disorientation for many people of color –in their encounter with some police officers today. How do we understand it? How do we fix it as concerned residents of Ferguson and beyond its borders? I don't really know. There is no one crystal ball. What I do observe, as logged in my diary is, that the problem can't be fixed by denying the implications of its existence: by denying – seemingly – the subtle reality of a "double standard" of response on the part of some police officers in dealing with black teens and white teens. Indeed, I suspect that these sort of conflicted perceptions need serous dialogue in the broader St. Louis community. Yet, a brief glimpse at Ferguson's interesting history – may shed some light on the situation of social unrest, in a land where "all of God's children" need sustainable jobs, respect, and equal opportunity to follow the American Dream.

1

Ferguson

A Historical Look

The intriguing question for me is simple as it is complex, namely, what is the historical landscape of Ferguson?

From a historical perspective, it was in the 1850s that William B. Ferguson—a true entrepreneurial spirit—agreed to deed a strip of land through his farm to the North Missouri Railroad, later known as the Wabash Railroad. Historically, this was done on the condition that they build a depot on this land and make it a regular stop. This stop, known as Ferguson Station, became the center of economic and social activity around the area; and Mr. Ferguson subdivided his land and sold lots to businesses and homeowners. By 1894, the population had reached 1,000 and the town of "Ferguson Station" was incorporated as a first class city.

To be sure, the city boomed during the Post-World War II era, anchored, in part, with new industries, including the relocated headquarters of Emerson Electric Company. Former slaves of Thomas January and other slaves freed after the Civil War contributed to the early establishment of a racially diverse population. Thus in 1954, Ferguson became a Charter City, one of the first in St. Louis County to adopt this council-manager form of government.[1] *In terms of population, the cross-cultural makeup of the city, in recent years, include approximately 65.2% black (13,840); it reflects 30.3% white (6,432).*

In 2012, the general population of the city of Ferguson was approximately 21,135 people living within its borders. In 2013, the comparative figure in the general population was approximately 21,111 people.[2] Historically, the depot and the "train engine whistle" played a significant and constructive role in the social, political, economic, and religious life of Ferguson. Looking forward as we reflect back in 2015, we need—as never before—a new "train engine whistle" to sound out the tunes of peace, justice, equal regard, mutual understanding, and systemic change in all aspects of human community. Yet, Ferguson is also layered with many strange images and conflicting narratives of St. Louis.

Notwithstanding, the critical visibility of race cuts deep into the funky facts of life—which underscores the historic racial divide in St. Louis between African Americans and Caucasians. For example, I have been persistently informed by many St. Louisians of the presence of so called "racial covenants" that once blanketed certain inner city and suburban neighborhoods and subdivisions. It seems that history is always partial to irony and surprise, in that the Missouri Compromise allowed slavery in Missouri in 1820. Just a year later, Missouri enters the union as a slave state (Jeannette Cooperman's essay "The Color Line," in magazine *St. Louis Black and White*, November, 2014).[3]

To fast forward almost a half-century, it was Chief Justice Roger B. Taney of Maryland, who ruled that "Dred Scott," a classic case of double standards, was not a citizen of Missouri within the meaning of the Constitution of the United States, and not entitled as such to sue in its courts; . . . Taney, in effect, stripped all African Americans of any legal standing as citizens of the United States; and subsequently declared, in regard to blacks as "so far inferior, that they had no rights which the white man was bound to respect."

1. Long, *Barack Obama of Thee I Sing*, 16–28.
2. Data Source: City of Ferguson, History, 63135.
3. Cooperman, "The Color Line," 70–71.

Unfortunately this perceived legal declaration of so called "black inferiority" –historically—set the dominant normative racial curve for the proper status of the "negro" for many decades to come, both in Missouri and around the cultural landscape of the nation.

This perennial racial divide is revealed in many facets of American life from *Plessey v. Ferguson* (1895); legal segregation initiative (1916) to black children permitted to swim in Fairgrounds Park, but whites resisted and riot breaks out (1949); to Attorney Frankie Freeman takes St. Louis Housing Authority to court and wins 1954); to protests outside Jefferson Bank to include white-collar workers of color (1963); to Jones v. Alfred H. Meyer Co. declaring racial discrimination in housing as illegal (1968);[4] to Freeman Bosley, Jr. elected as the 1st black mayor in St. Louis (1993); and fast forward to 2014 in the police shooting of Michael Brown, Jr. in Ferguson, on August 9, 2014. Ironically, it appears that whatever outlook ordinary people may have about the racial divide: the funky rhythms and beats go on.

Furthermore, expressions of hope and gradual recovery crop-up along the main avenue of W. Florissant in Ferguson—as ordinary folk find the courage to begin again. I am reminded always about the words of my father, a carpenter by trade, growing up in the Deep South, who muttered to his contemporaries concerning the virtue of courage in hard times:

> *Courage, brother or sister, do not stumble,*
> *Though your path seems dark as night;*
> *There is a star to guide the humble;*
> *Trust in God and do the right.*[5]

Therefore, I suspect that "sayings" from my father were gems of wisdom given to me. I also found these gems of wisdom in the Ferguson community to keep us grounded in the civility of common sense and social responsibility to be our "brother's keeper and not our brother's killer." Be that as it may, the path we choose

---

4. Ibid., 72.

5. J. Nathan Oglesby, St. James M.B. Church, Christian Education Conference, Earle Arkansas (1962).

is ours alone; but the consequences affect us all. As we stride for deeper understanding as American citizens, some of the sayings, which I observed in Ferguson, read:

"We are Still Here!"

"Our Faith in Ferguson will not
Fizzle before the finish!"

"We will Rebuild!"
"Business Owners are still struggling,
Lend a Helping Hand!"

2

Waves and Voices from the Otherside

> The problem of the twentieth century
> Is the problem of the Color Line.
> —W.E.B. DuBois

> There is neither Jew nor Greek,
> There is neither slave nor free,
> There is neither male nor female;
> For you are all one in Christ Jesus.
> —(Galatians 3:28)

With the twentieth century in our recent past, there is a profound irony and lingering memory by many Americans of the strange truth, apparently, inherent in this classic statement etched out by W.E.B. DuBois. Of course, the biblical citation points toward an alternative reality.

I know that we have made tremendous progress in regard to race and ethnic relations in America—especially since the birth of this original statement by Professor DuBois in *The Souls of Black Folk* (1903).[1] Here the moral dilemma of many young and old African Americans was keenly articulated back in the rhythmic flux of U.S. history. He said a word for us today to still ponder, although the popular language has changed. *"Am I an American or am I a Negro? . . . One ever feels his twoness,"* says DuBois – *"an American, a Negro . . . two warring ideals in one dark body.*[2]*"* I suspect for some ordinary folk in our culturally pluralistic society this dilemma is still unresolved. The perennial dilemma of skin-color has not fully gone away—despite the progressive achievements of the civil rights movement over five decades ago.

"Don't live in the past," said one of my white neighbors to me recently. However, it appears to me to echo a different narrative, in the release of The Grand Jury Decision, in the Michael Brown case, on November 24, 2014. I recall and observed, then the systemic and well-coordinated preparation by both state and local authorities to put down disturbances, burnings, and violence against persons and property. Yet the waves of unrest and violence did not go away into the night. It blooded the social climate, in the aftermath of the decision by the Grand Jury—composed of nine white citizens, and three black citizens, according to some local news media outlets. One wave of street protest, I observed, called the Grand Jury Decision, "outrageous, unfair, and a shame!"

Further, I observed that raw emotions ran high throughout North St. Louis and certain communities of St. Louis County. These disturbances and raw emotions by some protestors and ordinary folk do not, as I see it, negate whatever initiative made by state and local officials to rebuild broken lives and restore trust among hard working people in Ferguson.

Politically, for example, the fires and unrest caught the attention of the nation and world. Because history is partial to irony and surprise, where will the next wave of real help, in the interest

---

1 Du Bois, The Souls of Black Folk, 17
2. Ibid., 17–18.

of Ferguson, come from—both on the practical and political levels? Well, the answer could be among the "voices often ignored" or from passionately expressed voices less politically sophisticated and blindly optimistic.

For example, who could have imagined and believed, in the lifetime of humankind, the election of Barack Obama, as Commander-in-Chief—the first black president of the United States of America. For many tearful eyes of hope and promise, many black Christians deeply believe that God moves in mysterious ways. For many tearful eyes of promise, the dawn of a new day, suddenly, appeared. Why can't we embrace the waves and voices of the Ferguson movement? In my own diary, here are some reality-grounded stories, observations, and reflections I wrote down over the last year—and concretely, I remember many critical challenges as a resident of St. Louis County. Let us now take a closer look at waves of folk sayings from ordinary Americans that helped to shape my own understanding and ethical sensibility in regard to the Ferguson movement. In my personal diary, I logged certain re-vibrating chants by many peaceful protestors, who echoed deep concerns and sentiments of support for justice and fairness in the killing of Michael Brown, Jr.

As I observed, these were ordinary community people from all walks of life—some high school friends and classmates who knew Michael up close, some were area college students; some were church folk and religious practitioners, some community leaders with no particular theology or ideology, politicians and some priests. Some elderly and physically challenged—and voices that served notice from the U. S. Department of Justice from Attorney General Eric Holder to the Missouri Governor's office of Jay Nixon. In our common wealth of democracy, we have, apparently, touched the core values and heart of many ordinary citizens in our multi-ethnic society. Without a doubt, some of the sayings or chants I emphatically remember included the following:

1. "Hands up, Don't Shoot!"
2. "Hands up, Don't Shoot!"

3. "Black Lives Matter!"
4. "Black Lives Matter!"
5. "Black Lives Matter!"
6. "RAMS Hands Up!"
7. "RAMS Hands Up!"
8. "RAMS Hands Up!"
9. "I Love ♡ Ferguson"
10. "I Love ♡ Ferguson"
11. "I Love ♡ Ferguson"
12. "Do Something, Don't Let Injustice Win!"
13. "Do Something, Don't Let Injustice Win!"
14. "Do Something, Don't Let Injustice Win!"
15. "My Feet had almost slipped, had it not been for my brother's strong hand in the Ferguson Movement"
16. "From near and far, we come in Peace marching for Justice for Michael Brown"
17. "Without Justice, No Peace!"
18. "Stand up to Police brutality!"
19. "God is on our side!"
20. "From invisible faces in the jailhouse, to justice advocates in the courthouse!"
21. "Limited Peace can't get Unlimited Justice!"
22. "We Won't Stop!"
23. "Ferguson's power brokers convinced against their will, will keep holding on to old habits still."
24. From President Obama's White House, it's the American People's House of freedom!

25. Can Michael Brown's delayed legacy of justice really live? I'm gonna never know: Must I see it in Ferguson as America's New Jim Crow?
26. Sounds of police brutality must never overshadow ordinary folk's waves of love.
27. Without justice in the marketplaces, people of color in America have no place.
28. I've never seen a young teen that God couldn't use.
29. To be at peace with each other, links the destiny of teens and police officers as brothers.
30. Ferguson's protestors move forward with passion—and often without cash—other groups around the nation, followed with, a peace-marching dash!
31. The bond of listening to all of our youth, leads to the bridge of understanding each youth.
32. Confused and discontent teens often see cops as strange folk, who watch certain ones in the community; rather than watching-over the safety-of-community.
33. If teens of color are regarded by some cops as mere rabbits; I hear some people say: "it ain't no fun when the rabbits got the guns!"
34. Yet, I believe that anti-police sentiment or violence cannot be tolerated by any of us—despite mistrust and neighborhood brokenness.
35. The fragile moral fabrics of our neighborhoods can only be built-up by us all.
36. The police body-cam, I think, is not an option but a necessity—for public safety.
37. The police body—cam is only a first functional step—for public safety and the safety of our police officers.
38. What we, perhaps need is no crabby attitude, but lofty aptitudes in regard to ethnic relations in America.

39. What we need is oneness—i.e., the capacity to listen, understand and, to show kindness and justice along the way (Micah 6:8).

40. In my own community, Ferguson or beyond: less than my best is failure if I don't work for a peace that begins with ME.

41. Less than my best is failure if I don't work for justice that begins with ME.

42. In my own community, black or white: less than my best is failure if I can't passionately follow the path of peace and justice (Amos 5:22–24; Matt. 5:9).

43. In my own community, black or white: less than my best is failure if I don't work for better human relations.

44. In my own community, black or white: less than my best is failure if I don't work for nonviolence, safe streets, and safe schools.

45. In my own community, black or white: less than my best is failure if I don't encourage children to work for excellence in both public and private education

46. (Prov 21:6). "No trials, no treasures."

47. In my own community, mixed, multicultural, multiethnic, gay, lesbian, transgender or straight: less than my best is failure if I don't value the other as an expression of God's love and favor in the world (John 3:16).

48. In my own community, Christian or non-Christian: less than my best is failure if I don't embrace the simple vision that God has made from one blood all the peoples of the Earth (Ps 8:4–5).

49. In my own community, Ferguson or beyond: less than my best is failure if I don't work diligently—for making the values of justice, trust, and healing between our teens and police officers a reality.

50. Ultimately, whether living in Ferguson or beyond: the reality of the "I—consciousness" is never separated from

"We—consciousness" (Mt 18:20). The bottom line is: we pull-together for a better tomorrow. (Rev 22:1, 4).

51. You drive me out with a stick, I'll come back with my own stick; but if you drive me out with the truth: We both can live in freedom (John 8:32).

52. Where there are dwelling places of justice, peace itself is created in communities like Ferguson.

53. Non-violence among us all, therefore, must not be a convenient option—but a way of life (Ps 29:11; Is 9:6; Is 32:17 cf).

54. Non-violence is not a shield for weak folk, but a mighty fortress for ordinary folk of character and courage.

55. It is not only the Ferguson movement that stirs our passion, but the passion, for justice that stirs our faith and action (James 2:17–18).

56. Tough-love is not an option, to be dismantled at one's convenience.

57. Tough-love is a healing word between parents and children, between gang members and gang drop-outs, and between peacemakers and law-makers.

58. Tough-love is a fancy word for justice in all places for all people—in all cases. (Ps 103:6; Hos 12:6).

59. Whether you are Red, Yellow, Black or White—a "snatch-and-grab" attitude will not get you to the path of educational excellence and aptitude (2 Tim 2:15).

60. Whether young protestors or adults—whose passions fill the streets of Ferguson, or elsewhere—when you climb the mountain of success, throw down ropes, not scissors, that others, too, might climb!

61. Peace, without justice, is like celebrating the groom in a wedding without the bride.

62. Peacemakers know that peace itself is not the absence of community tensions, but the presence of moral strength.

63. Dwelling places of peace are found in the hearts of ordinary folk committed to do battle for justice.
64. To paraphrase the famous words of Martin Luther King, Jr., "One must not be judged by the color of one's skin . . . Yet I believe that the greater virtue of all is: "To Love the skin you are in!"
65. For human beings the world over, the path where the virtues of love and mercy will meet—is justice.
66. In the Ferguson movement, who will sound the trumpet for our children's future—black or white—and other shades of ethnicity?
67. A telescope through which we look at the future must not, necessarily, be the lens of the rich and famous—but the homeless and helpless ones.
68. Burdens of the day find sweet rest, in the bosoms of ordinary folk—while reclining upon the chair of inner peace.
69. True peace always comforts the afflicted; and afflicts the comfortable.
70. In the continuing struggles of Ferguson, deep is the hunger for oneness over "broken places" in community: true security lives in the shout, "We Won't Quit!"

Note:

Pragmatically, I logged in my diary—especially in above numbers 24-60—some of my own critical reflections in regard to protestors and voices in the streets of Ferguson about the actual struggle for peace and justice.

3

Waves of White Anger vs. Black Response

> Prejudice is the devil unchained.
> —Charles W. Chestnut, American Novelist

> Simon, Simon, take heed: Satan has been given leave to sift all of you like wheat; but for you I have prayed that your faith may not fail. . . .
> —Luke 22:31–32 (NEB)

I have found among my Anglo-American students and friends that racial prejudice is, undoubtedly, an uncomfortable topic of conversation—either in the classroom or in the streets of our multi-ethnic society. As Duchess de Abrantes once remarked: "Prejudice squints when it looks, and lies when it talks."[1] Ironically, it is hard to find a happy medium in the context of American cul-

---

1. de Abrantes, *The New Dictionary of Thoughts*, 513.

ture. Prejudice—from whatever social group in the rainbow of skin color—is not so much dependent upon natural law, but upon learned habits, and traditions, consciously or unconsciously, that we internalize day-by-day. Here I suspect that racial prejudice is, sometimes, ignorantly, blind. Other times, it can be boldly blatant and intentional. In any case, it hurts, steals, and kills the threads of our common humanity—whether American, Jewish, Christian or non-Christian, African, Arab, Gay, Straight, Latino, Physically and mentally challenged, rich or poor, adult or child—and whatever threads of the human condition.

For many hard-core realists, however, racial prejudice is entrenched in the DNA, metaphorically speaking, of our predominantly white institutions and social customs. But the struggle of the moral person asks the questions, *"Is constructive change possible in the trenches of unrest in Ferguson communities and beyond?" How ought we to respond to the painful and funky facts of life as etched in the Ferguson Movement?* These and other questions cannot be easily answered—without honest dialogue and openness to our own biases, wounds, racial insecurities, and memory.

William Wells Brown, a 19th century American novelist once remarked, *"We are what we remember."* In the rhythm of my own memory—while living in St. Louis County in a middle class neighborhood—I purchased a new house, built from the ground up. To the surprise of some folk, we were the first African American family to live on this predominantly white block. All of our neighbors—with the exception of two growing Latino families—were white.

For example, I clearly remember, to my surprise, a morally disturbing incident that involved a county police officer—who subsequently received a frantic call from a white woman, living on our block saying: *"I saw a black man walking on my own street . . . just peeping in cars . . . so please check it out right away!"* Well, I actually live on the same street; and it was my regular custom to walk around the block for mere exercise after work, in the neighborhood. Concretely, I had not peeped into anybody's car. Personally, I shared with the police officer that not only had I not been a "car-peeping-Tom," but rather I had two new cars in my own garage! To be sure, the county police officer was polite—after I voluntarily showed him my I.D. and driver's license. For reasons I cannot honestly and fully explain but peculiar to the black experience in America, I always carry some form of I.D. while walking or jogging.

In our own family, for instance, we are blessed to have two sons. As parents, we did, in fact teach our children the value of respect for all people—especially "extra" respect to police officers: for they carry the "lethal heat"—and "young man," I would seriously say, "one perceived wrong movement or misunderstanding could quickly get out of hand!" This is not a Hollywood fiction, but a fact, that often reflects the unspoken burden many black fathers and mothers in America carry—both in their heart as well as their head.

Again, the poignant words of William Wells Brown—namely "We are what we remember"—are cogently relevant to the current situation of racial unrest in the Ferguson Movement. Even in allegedly professional circles, the racial factor appears to be—always—*the white elephant in the room.* Now, I suspect that a second true story may illustrate this fact. The glaring story that I remember—which never faded from of own academic and professional self-conscious—involved my teaching in a local graduate school in St. Louis County, as a full-time professor of social ethics.

For better or worse, I am a person of color. Well accepted by most white colleagues, I lived initially in a "glass-house!" At least, by one of my beloved white colleagues—Prof. Richard Lewis Scheef, Jr.,[2] whom I trusted, as he told me true riveting stories of him marching for social justice and racial integration, in Selma Alabama with Dr. Martin Luther King, Jr. and other civil rights protestors.

Of course, I was radically humble by his own commitment to racial equality, freedom, and the sacred worth of human personality. Joyfully, we often would talk long into the night about mutually critical issues—as friends and colleagues—in our society.

2. Scheef, White civil rights activist.

In any event, I remember being called, suddenly, into the office of President Robert Fauth—regarding a certain Board member, of our institution, who doubted the academic legitimacy of my earned Ph. D degree from Boston University.

Without hesitation—but feeling morally outraged—I was advised to prove—it. So then, in the speed of breathe I immediately, requested an official copy of my Ph. D transcript to be placed in the president's office, in order to accommodate that skeptical Board member. I never knew his name!

Meanwhile, I shared this incident with most of my white colleagues. I boldly inquired with many in these words, "were any of you subjected to the same strict academic rules of discourse of such a Board member's mandate?" They were not. Undoubtedly, I felt pain, hurt, and at times marginalized—but I never had a desire to give-up on my dreams or the support that many of my white colleagues provided—despite the particularity of skin-color. I remember also the powerful words of a pivotal educator—who taught Martin Luther King, Jr., at Morehouse College, in Atlanta, Georgia—Benjamin E. Mays, who sometimes told his colleagues and students as he muttered:

> *Fleecy locks and dark complexion*
> *Cannot forfeit nature's claim;*
> *Skin may differ*
> *But intellect and affection*
> *Run in black and white the same.*[3]

Historically, the reality of skin-color, whether "dark complexion" or "high yellow," has been one of America's most significant cultural problems—regardless of the patterns of racial unrest in Ferguson or in New York City, or in the struggle to live in other parts of the country. Because of racism and its subsequent patterns of colorism in our multi-ethnic society, we tend to subsist on the uneasy edges of the racial divide. In this sense, Ferguson, as I observe it, is not essentially different from other major municipalities around the nation, seeking to grapple with young teens of color, on

---

3. Mays, *Society for the Study of Black Religion.*

the one hand; and police officers, on the other. Yet, the problematic of what some ordinary folk call the "color-thing" needs to be critically understood and dismantled. For many ordinary folk, who struggle to survive and deal with the funky facts of life daily—the so called "color-thing" can be expressive of this saying:

> *If you are white, you're alright;*
> *If you are brown, stick around;*
> *If you are yellow, you're mellow;*
> *But if you are black, get back!*

Notwithstanding, how easy it is for us to forget that Dr. Martin Luther King, Jr. warned us and the entire global community that a *"man must not be judged by the color of his skin, but by the content of his character."* Here I think that he was getting at the difficulty problem of colorism in the modern world; and how it can be so easily subverted and manipulated to make one group of people feel that they are better or superior to another group of people—simply by the color of one's skin. Indeed, I think that the funky facts of life in the Fergusons around every urban center in our great nation tend to reflect the values and painful legacy of this slippery narrative.[4]

For ordinary people of African descent, the average child grows up in America with what I call a "double-barrel-dilemma." By this, I mean to suggest, that the child is often dubbed by society with the label "black"—in some cultural or statistical form. So, the first dilemma—psychologically is the mind of a child or adult and what that really means. The second dilemma in the barrel—metaphorically—in the term "color," and the subsequent values often attached to it in the broader context of Western culture.

Whether you live in Ferguson or elsewhere in our global society, the word "black"—as opposed to "white"—is associated with the negatives, such as: black ball, black magic, black market, a black mark, black list, black looks, dirty, pertaining to "the utterly dismal gloom," and expressions of that which is "outrageously wicked." By contrast, the word "white"—etymologically—reflects positive

---

4. Oglesby, "Unpublished Paper."

expressions or ascribed values such as, "pure, innocent, harmless, fortunate, honesty, square-dealing, honorable" and that which reflects the "achromatic color of highest brilliance." According to *Webster's New International Dictionary*, comparatively speaking, these were the dominant functional definitions and understandings inherent—conspicuously—in the above words.

Ethically, I strongly believe that the "black-thing" and the "color-thing" are latent and perennial factors in the Ferguson Movement, as well as the society at large. They tend to bear witness to the tensions and uneasiness of the social and racial divide: they point toward communal brokenness and confusion over certain words like black or white, because they may remind us of complex realities in our multiethnic culture. For instance, I have served for many years as Professor of social ethics and as an ordained minister in St. Louis County, for over three decades. Ironically, the difficult issue of colorism, is one I find both joyfully amazing and odd. For example, out of all of the weddings, which I officiated formally—I have not married a bride who requested to walk down the church aisle in a black wedding gown. I observe that NEVER! NEVER! NEVER! did it ever happen in black. Be that as it may, these sort of real-life events say a lot about the power of colorism, even today.

From the perspective of my own personal narrative, I actually grew up in the northeastern city of Earle, Arkansas. I vividly remember as a teenager of the 1960s how sensitive classmates were around the question of "colorism." For example, Chester (17 years old) and his younger brother Roy (14 years old) seem to always start a fuss. Now in the community of my teenage years, they were my next door neighbors. As brothers, Chester often would tease Roy by ribbing him with these words, "you are the black sheep of the family. . . ." Of course little Roy felt bad and hurt by his older brother. Blackness, I remember, was not the sound Roy wanted to hear!

Another true story from the community of my childhood that I remember is about the "double-barrel dilemma" of colorism—affecting black girls in particular. It was the strange belief that "light-skin" girls were more beautiful than "dark-skin" girls, who grew up into womanhood. Accordingly, I remember how some girls in high school would attempt to "lighten" their skin color. In this strange social process, many of the neighborhood girls would use a commercial product call, "Bleach and Glow"—chemically based facial cream known to lighten one's skin. Secretly, everybody knew, seemingly, what was going on. I shared these two true stories, because they underscore the continuing complex problem of colorism today. Furthermore, they implicitly or explicitly connect us to the ongoing-problem of the color-line in the Ferguson Unrest. With the in-group "rap" of black folk themselves, the self-defeating and harsh negative saying of some was: "the lighter, the brighter!" In short, two critical questions beg for space in our deliberations and reflections. First, it seems to me that for members of the in-group, should certain African Americans still harbor—young or adult, overtly or covertly—in their bosom, apparently for some, the dream to be light-skin? Secondly, a general pragmatic question that comes to mind, in the painful drama of the Ferguson unrest, must include rioters and peace-breakers themselves. Accordingly, what responsibility rioters must play in re-building the scarred walls of Ferguson? However, in our continuing effort to explore the issues of colorism, white anger, and black moral rage—we have attempted to unpack, in part, the so called "double-barrel dilemma" peculiar to the black experience in America. With no pun intended, it ain't easy being "black" in America today—with its own strangely twisted logic of colorism, just knocking on the doors of ordinary folk in the countless Fergusons around the country.

Perhaps, the best recipe of cross-cultural rhythms in regard to our health and diversity, over the last four decades, was the emergence of the black consciousness movement involving such iconic personalities as Aretha Franklin, James Brown, Maya Angelou, Toni Morrison, Alice Walker, Nina Simone, Howard Thurman, Stokely Carmichael, Rosa Parks, Coretta Scott King, Fannie Lou Hamer—to name just a few. On the critical question of colorism, and the struggle for viable interpretations of blackness in the twenty first century, I have been captivated –in part—by the two amazing icons in soul music. The classic Queen of Soul, Aretha Franklin, in her funky lyrics *R.E.S.P.E.C.T*; and the resounding normative resolve of children, teens, and adults of African descent to be sun kissed by God—in a fragrance of beauty and self-acceptance. For example, the classic lyric of James Brown, in my opinion, expresses this powerful sentiment in the song: *"Say it Loud, I'm Black and I'm Proud!"*

Yet, these deep issues of the head and heart—locked into the rhythmic flux of life—command serious perennial attention on various sides of the color line.

As a resident of St. Louis County—peculiar to my own observations and experiences—Ferguson, I believe, is a tight knitted community of decent and hardworking folk, who are passionate fighters for their individual and collective versions of peace and justice, responsibility and reciprocity, and the longing urge for healing and hospitality.[5] *(Source: Please note that the above literary observations were logged in my diary on the eve of Martin Luther King, Jr. Holiday in St. Louis, MO, January 18, 2015).*

It is more than a glimpse into the obvious, to discern the normative racial stereotypes negatively entrenched in this often used "saying" that "to look black, is to be ugly." It is painfully offensive to me. But in the waves of funky rhythms on the stormy sea of the racial divide in Ferguson, I have heard about this "color-thing" several times—for better or worst.

Paradoxically, the number one reason why this "color-thing" needs empirical scrutiny is the fact that it is not true. For example, it is my view as a participant-observer that many peace-protestors were and are passionate believers in social justice—in behalf of young Michael Brown, Jr. in particular—made up of every color in the human rainbow: that is to say, some were black marchers, white marchers, Latino, Asian, young and old, preachers and politicians, gay and transgender, community activists and economic organizers, educators and engineer college students—to name just a few.

5. Oglesby, Personal Diary.

Waves of White Anger vs. Black Response

Metaphorically, it is my observation that the reality of white-anger—on the other side of the track—was swifted and forthright. Fear and rage were also present since day-one (August 9th 2014), as Michael Brown's body laid on the street for over four hours. Local authorities and media outlets reported a rapid increase, in some St. Louis County municipalities, of gun sales! Here it seems to me—as recorded in my personal diary—there was a growing "uneasiness between black folk and white folk." Hard to grasp, I felt like something bad and calamitous forces had broken out all around certain neighborhoods in Ferguson—like a tidelwave of agony and anger.

Indeed, I observed and experienced the presence of raw anger on both sides of the color-line. For example, with many African Americans who peacefully live in St. Louis, it was the anger of disbelief and moral rage over the tragic killing of Michael Brown, Jr., in a relatively uneventful day in the hot month of August, 2014—where floods of goodhearted fans tend to come from many parts of the Mid-West to enjoy the fun-filled fruits of Cardinal baseball. By contrast, I suspect and observed that "white anger" came from a different direction and cultural location. Unlike the web of "black moral rage"—which tends to be steeped in unresolved centuries of economic powerlessness and oppression—the mantle of "white anger," as I observed some expressions in Ferguson, is nothing less than the arrogance of power, often taking the forms of heavy duty street tanks and the over-militarization of the community. I saw and experienced this inward anguish as I became emotionally stunned by the enormous display of police and military presence—in what we ironically and rightly celebrate, as "The Land of the Free and the Home of the Brave!" in the context of American society.

Moreover, it may be well for us to pause and remember that the "white anger" and "black moral rage" have been around on the contemporary American scene for quite some time in multiethnic relations. Historically, these conflicted impulses seem to be rooted in patterns of both *defacto* segregation (i.e., based on housing restrictions, restrictive covenants, keeping blacks from buying white personal property), and *de jure* segregation (i.e., the patterns of segregation by law). In any event, I suspect that ordinary folk of conscience would—reasonably—admit that the conflicting impulses of "white anger" and "black rage" are important factors in the Ferguson unrest. Undoubtedly, the critical dilemma of the arrogance of power has been illustrated by many scholars, educators, community activists, leaders, teachers, preachers and politicians. Perhaps, few thinkers, in my opinion, have dealt with this critical dilemma more eloquently than Martin Luther King, Jr. as he boldly asserted that the real dilemma inherent in the arrogance of power, in regards to peaceful protestors and justice-seekers in American, is the basic struggle between the forces of "immoral power and powerless morality" in our society.

What is at stake, here, for Ferguson's viability and community rebuilding seem to revolve, in part, around what King referred to as a triadic relationship between: a) poverty, b) prejudice, and c) prophetic witness. For his own social analysis, these components are not by any means static and separate; rather they are dynamic and interdependent—whether in the Ferguson unrest, or other urban centers born in the fire of racial division. Given the socio-economic realities of Ferguson, patterns of mis-trust and racial division are often triggered by what may be described as Anglo-phobia and Afro-phobia. For example, the former notion refers essentially—to a fear of people of European descent. The latter notion tends to refer to a fear of people—essentially—of African descent. Obviously, they are issues of gray and an amazing array of complexity among all multi-ethnic groups in Ferguson and beyond. As the humorist H. L. Menchen once remarked, *"For every difficult and complex issue, there is always an answer that's simple, easy, and wrong!"*

Now in the early throws of Ferguson's riots and unrest, I logged in the diary—the offensive smells of racism despite the promise of a color blind society. Of course, it is very easy to turn one's head and look the other way. Even more problematic at times, is the impulse of denial. Maybe not for all, but for some, the phenomenon of racism in America is still alive and well—despite progressive civil rights laws of the past four decades. While some ordinary folk would not agree with the posture of Jim Wallis, a noted activist for peace in a justice, that racism is America's original Sin. "Perhaps Jim Wallis was, indeed, calling for a sort of "social confession" to the reality of racism as a continuing factor in American life—whether we live in Ferguson, New York City, Cleveland or other places in our society. By the term "racism"— which is very emotionally complex and hard to define—I mean to suggest the interlocking triadic relationship between a) race prejudice, usually associated with strong feelings of ethnic superiority; b) plus power, and c) plus privileges peculiar to being a member of the white community.

Therefore, whether one lives in the geopolitical township of Ferguson or other municipalities of the county, racism is a topic that so many people duck or remain silent—especially in St. Louis' white community. Yet the "color line" and the ugly scare of racial segregation persist in some parts of St. Louis. In terms of economic or social disparity, the critical question is this—namely—"what are the funky facts of life in St. Louis, in regard to the Black-White divide?"

Here again, what I found insightful and cogently relevant was Jeannette Cooperman's empirical description of "class and race" in St. Louis vis-a-vis the nation. For example, she observed the following facts for us to chew on:

> St. Louis is one of the 10 most segregated
> Metropolitan areas in the nation.
> If African-Americans live in the city,
> They often live in North City.[6]

> More than three-quarters of the
> County's 90 municipalities remain
> More than 80 percent white' or black.

> For children in the St. Louis area in 2000,
> The rate of exposure to neighborhood
> Poverty was approximately 22 percent

---

6. "Class and Race," St. Louis Black and White, 74.

African-Americans and 7 percent Caucasians.

*St. Louis is 39th in the nation in
Upward mobility, largely due to the
Concentration of low income families.*[7]

To be sure, the Ferguson's riots demonstrated to me the awesome ethical burden of digging into the funky facts of life—both economically and socially. Ferguson's unrest also illustrated the complex forms of racism in America—and how they are tied to the issues of power and prejudice.

Comparatively speaking, therefore, we may observe a more functional definition of racism that emerged in Joseph Barndt's volume, *Dismantling Racism: The Challenge to White America*. He argues, and I think rightly so, that racism goes beyond mere prejudice.[8] Any person or member of a given ethnic group can, in fact, be prejudice. "Prejudice" means pre-judgment which leads to "mis-judgment"—whether that person be Euro-American, Asian, Latino, Native-American, or African-American—just to name a few. But the phenomenon of racism, according to Barndt, is by definition radically different. For Barndt, "Racism is prejudice plus power." He argues for the distinction in this manner:

Everyone is prejudiced, but not everyone is racist. To be prejudiced means to have opinions without knowing the facts. . . . to be racially prejudiced means to have distorted opinions about people of other races. Racism goes beyond prejudice. It is backed up by power. Racism is the power to enforce one's prejudices.[9]

In terms of the perennial observation and analysis of the wider problem of racism in America, nobody gets off the hook—whether you are black or white—whether you live in St. Louis, in Ferguson or beyond its borders. It seems to me that we all have a lot at stake to eliminate the odorous smell of racism itself—from the cracks of our common life, for the healing of hurts, for the

---

7. Ibid., 74.
8. Barndt, Dismantling Racism, 25–30
9. Ibid., 28.

bonds of peace and justice, and the building bridges of trust between police officers and black teens in particular.

To be ethically honest, these realities and stories about prejudice and power are not unique to St. Louis or the culture of Ferguson. They can be, easily, multiplied a million times over in countless urban center and communities of color in our Democratic Republic. Therefore, let waves of white anger consider <u>angles</u> of <u>vision</u> and courage to walk in the shoes of the other—regardless of the rhythmic flux of the Ferguson unrest. What follows from my diary is a limited sharing of some sayings, observations, and reflections along the way—as a resident of St. Louis County:

1. "Back the Police!"
2. "Never mind about things, they get what they deserve!"
3. In St. Louis, agonize over what else must abide in order to save us now from the tragic 2014 stat of 159 homicides?
4. Healing comes only when Peace-Protestors and Police-Officers are on the S.A.M.E. P.A.G.E.
5. Understanding comes only when Police-Officers and Peace-Protestors are on the S.A.M.E. P.A.G.E.
6. "We don't go around with sagging pants, and all that anger inside!"
7. "Why don't you-people stop complaining and get a job like everybody else."
8. "You can start by getting off welfare!"
9. "We Back The Badge!"
10. "In America, in our great country, we all have the same opportunity, the same hours in the day!"
11. "You call me "racist" You are the racist ones—not me!"
12. You don't see Mexicans crossing the border resisting arrest, when they get caught!"
13. "They come here to work!"

14. "All you (Blacks) do is crime!"
15. "Try working for a change!"
16. "Protest the black criminal record."
17. "The ones where they, (blacks), are number one is in killing other blacks."
18. "They, (blacks), are number one in high school dropouts!"
19. "They, (blacks), are number one in welfare and food stamps."
20. "They, (blacks), are number one in not knowing about how a belt works on their baggy pants!"
21. "Think of all the Asians and Hispanics who come to this country and blew by them, (blacks), in all categories."
22. "Yet, the blacks are real problems for all the rest of us!"
23. "They, (blacks), are truly the number one racists!"
24. Some ordinary folk say, "I've never seen a bigot that God didn't love!"
25. Could it be: there is so much good in the worst of us; so much bad in the best of us, so who can tell the rest of us?
26. Strangely, the common enemy of humankind is not us: but the yoke of greed, selfishness, hypocrisy, self-deception, inequality, poverty, disease, revenge, and the absence of freedom (Gal 5:1).
27. We all are humankind.
28. Privileged groups seem to be more tempted by the insidious impulse to say, "We and They."
29. Peace protestors from whatever village in America, therefore, seem to know the wisdom in saying, "We are all in this mess together!"
30. A young child, living in Ferguson, asked his father, "Daddy. . . why so much mess? How do I now spell success?" The father simply but painfully replied, "Persistent effort, my child. . . Persistent effort!"

31. Why must we be estranged from each other by racial stereotypes—either in Ferguson, Missouri or countless Fergusons around the nation?

32. "Protest leaders from St. Louis have travelled," says John Gaskin III, a local community advocate for social justice,—"to cities like New York to provide leadership, motivation, and direction."

33. "I can't breathe."

34. "I can't breathe."

35. "I can't breathe."

36. Protest across the nation sheds light not on yesteryears' deeds, but bring attention to issues of excessive force by some U.S. Police Departments.

37. Law enforcement works best, when the community works diligently to repair bridges of mis-trust, as communities of Ferguson and North St. Louis attempt to heal old wounds.

38. God breaks in the wilderness of our own violence, only when I allow violence itself to unchain its grip on me.

39. Metaphorically speaking, some folk say, "God has no hands to work for the cause of justice, but our hands; no feet to walk the path of lasting peace but our feet." Therefore, be at peace with each other.

40. God's train of peace and justice just pulled—in on track nine into Ferguson, (for example, the 'train' symbolizing August 9, 2014, in the killing of Michael Brown, Jr.), and God commands all people to get-on-board! (Ps 146:7–9; Matt 5:9).

41. "Respect" is just another word, if we have gang members shooting other gang members, and innocent children in St. Louis' streets.

42. "I, too, love, Ferguson and our neighborhoods; but I don't accept what looters and thugs did to our businesses," says one local business owner.

43. One hunting protestor in the street crowd shouted, "I can't trust a preacher anymore than a politician!"
44. "We want peace, not protest! Our pain is so deep, even the doctor can't fix it," says one elderly man.
45. "Something gotta give; there must be a better way than burning, stealing, and throwing bottles at our police officers," shouted a community activist from North City.
46. "The blame game is not on us: you blacks are the real racists!"
47. We (whites) don't think all cops are bad cops."
48. "You black people don't really know the difference!"
49. "I feel, you'll get what you deserve."
50. "In America, there are no free rides. You people are always looking for a welfare handout!"
51. There may be mis-fit toys, but must we say: "they are, you know, just mis-fit people living in the ghetto!"
52. "Black people, you get over it. There are no free rides in our country."
53. "If you want the American Dream, you got to track it down; nobody is gonna give it to anybody lazy!"
54. "What about you folks, working for the American Dream—like all the rest of us do?"
55. "Stop blaming us for your problems, blame yourself."
56. "Police body cameras will help keep you'll in check, from doing all those drive-by shootings."
57. "Why do I see so much on TV, of your black teenagers breaking into our stores and businesses?"
58. Some ordinary folk seem to believe that the best way to ease Ferguson's racial unrest is the absence of racial injustice.
59. Most folk I know in the Ferguson Movement want more absence of police brutality; and less absence of police—community mis-trust.

Waves of White Anger vs. Black Response

60. Guess what? I suspect that some of these sentiments and attitudes can be observed in countless villages and cities around the landscape of our great American democracy.
61. The battle for justice did not begin with "just-us," but with sages and slaves who toiled hundreds of years ago, in this land.
62. The battle for justice, as a child of God, grows out of the amazing experience of the Sacred.
63. The battle for justice is never seeing your innocent children cry bad tears of pain or declare: "*There is nothing here in America to gain!*"
64. When I consider the deep water of the racial divide in America, "I ponder, who among us has the courage to SWIM?"
65. The battle for a new beginning—begins with "us" *not* "them."
66. The "us" *not* "them," always begins with we-together can make a difference.
67. We-together can change riot-torned streets—dripping with confusion, anger, and violence—into a venue of reconstruction and reconciliation.
68. It is not white-anger that hurts, but white-indifference to black suffering.
69. The only way out of the Fergusons around the world—is a compassionated-hand—into the messiness of rebuilding.
70. Every impulse of courage rides on the wing of community initiatives and self-responsibility.

4

Waves of Lament and Hope

> Hope is like the sun, which,
> As we journey toward it,
> Casts the shadow of
> Our burden behind us.
> —S. Smiles

> We do not raise our hands to the void
> For things beyond hope.
> – Rabindenath Tagore

> Let not those who hope in thee,
> O Lord, be put ashamed.
> —Ps 69:6

Waves of Lament and Hope

John Gaskin III, the youngest person from St. Louis ever elected to the NAACP's national board of directors, echoed the view of political involvement at the grassroots of community life. He then expressed the old saying, *"If you're not at the table, you're not on the menu."* Therefore, Gaskin emphasized that "voting counts!" Another voice that sounded the trumpet in the iconic Ferguson protest—with focus on education—was the voice of John Danforth, III, who held the view that *"Every child deserves hope, and black and white has nothing to do with it."*[1] (St. Lbw. p82 Nov. 20, 2014).

To be sure, there are many ways to move forward in the path of peace, racial-justice. But front lines along the path to the future are marked by the twin brothers of "Lament and Hope." Maybe nestled in the promise of hope, humans must struggle through the wilderness of "lament." Poetically, it seems to be reflective of the journey through the wilderness of pain to embrace a wave of justice and freedom unchained in the human spirit. Indeed, the language of "hope" unchains the broken spirit, and unmasks the struggle for oneness as we dare to dream beyond the pain. Poetically, consider these musings of my own inward toil:

> Unmasking the Pain
> In the struggle to discover
> Who I really am,
> I uncover my own pain.
> Could it be that when
> I am in the most pain
> I am most free?
> It's been said
> And many believe
> There can be no true gain,
> Without some pain,
> No hope with hardship.
>
> When I unmask my
> Own blackness in
> White America,
> I discover deep pain in
> The pit of my soul.

1. Danforth, "Education For All," St. Louis Black and White, 82

> Is there really a balm in Gilead
> To heal the wounded soul?
> I cannot tell.
>
> Beyond the transitory
> Pain of bitter prejudice and false pride
> There is power, power in
> My beautiful blackness;
> Power to affirm and to create;
> Power to resist and to inspire;
> Power to be pro-black
> Without being anti-white, or anti-semitic.[2]

To be sure, I have observed and discovered the struggle to "unmask" the reality of pain in the head and heart of Ferguson's residents of African descent is most acute. The struggle itself appears to be endless. However, peace protestors, who are committed to the long journey for social justice, seem to take comfort in the moral imperative laid down by Frederick Douglass over one hundred and fifty years ago, namely:

> *If there is no struggle, there*
> *is no progress. . . . This struggle*
> *may be a moral one, or it may be*
> *a physical one, or it may be both*
> *moral and physical, but it must be*
> *A struggle. Power concedes nothing*
> *without a demand.*[3]

In the heat of moral protest for the common good in Ferguson and around the nation, the burden of "lament" must not overshadow the goals of justice, peace, and mutual understanding. There must always be continuing struggle, if justice is to increase, and violence decrease in our families, villages, and neighborhoods. If we struggle to live, we live together. If we die, we still do not die alone, because the "voices" of justice ride on the whirlwind and on the storms of tomorrow. While weeping through the countless nights of the Ferguson unrest, the bitter-sweet irony of

2. Oglesby, "Unmasking the Pain," 86–87.
3. Newman, African American Quotations, 346–47.

the "lament" bears witness to the inevitability that tomorrow will come!

Biblically, I suspect that this is a deeper and practical meaning behind what some scholars as well as ordinary folk believe to be strangely relevant to the funky facts of life—especially among those who feel in their gut victimized by racial oppression and economic marginalization while living in Ferguson.

Now on the other hand, the language of "hope" involves the courage-to-be. Undoubtedly, the courage-to-be itself involved nothing less than a wave of peaceful voices speaking out for justice in the shooting death of Michael Brown, Jr. on August 9, 2014, by police officer Darren Wilson. In the course of events, the general public anxiously awaits the results from the Grand Jury, which was finally announced by Bob McCulloch, the St. Louis County Prosecutor on the evening of November 24, 2014, declaring police officer Darren Wilson innocent of all alleged charges in the case. Pursuant to the case itself, the U.S. Attorney General Eric Holder, meanwhile, launched his own investigation more broadly in regard to possible civil charges; but on January 22, 2015, it was announced that officer Wilson was not accountable to a civil rights violation, in the case of Michael Brown, Jr.

It is more than a glimpse into the obvious to observe a cloud of disbelief and moral outrage about the Grand Jury itself—being made up of nine whites and three blacks. Many peace protestors quietly went home, wrapped in the garment of melancholy. Many peace breakers roamed the urban and county streets, wrapped in the garments of anger, violence, lootings, and burnings. Apparently, many of these peaceful protestors—as I observed and anguished—were temporarily silenced. For example, I find it interesting that many community leaders took the opposite path of silence: the courage to speak, struggle, and plant seeds of understanding—while dealing with the funky facts of racial bigotry. Rev. Traci Blackmon, a pastor and activist, for instance, muttered these words, "*The real culprit in Ferguson . . . is racism, because the systematic oppression of African Americans is nothing new.*"[4]

---

4. Blackmon, St. Louis Black and White, 76.

It is profoundly interesting to me that the "lament" or "The book of Lamentations" in the Bible reflects, for instance, one dominant theme: communal sadness. The common theme here is the agony of the people—referring historically to Israel, and the power of a just and compassionate God to forgive and to restore brokenness (Lamentations chs. 1–5 cf). As the psalmist cry out for restoration, healing, and deliverance—perhaps the functional measuring rod for us who love Ferguson today is the need to create hospitable places of listening, learning, restoration and compassion for the other. As the Bible retorts:

> "Restore us to yourself, O Lord, that we may be restored; renew our days as of old—unless you have utterly rejected us, and are angry with us beyond measure"

—(Lam 5:21–22).

In any event, the language of the "lament" has, as it were, many interpretative shades and ethical implications in our observation of the Ferguson Movement.

In this last formal literary discourse—reflecting the dynamic themes of "Lament and Hope"—I wish to return, for a moment, to shed conceptual light on the importance of keeping a diary and how I value it, and as a way to better understand the racial divide as well as to grapple with resurgent patterns of racism around the nation.

Now the *American College Dictionary* uses the term "diary" to refer to the writer's own observations and experiences in regard to keeping a daily record of some kind. It is a word derived, therefore, from the Latin term <u>diarium</u>, meaning daily allowance or journal."[5] By contrast, *The Dictionary of Cultural Literary* refers to "diary" as intentional observation and experiences of a certain group's customs.[6] Some observations as a resident of St. Louis County will be, in part, forthcoming—as citizens of the "RED, WHITE & BLUE" banner is not purely a black-white problem. It is not purely a moral problem. But it is, seemingly—on one level of

---

5. Barnhart, ed., American College Dictionary, 334.
6. Hirsch, Dictionary of Cultural Literacy, 397

human discourse—an epistemological problem. By this I mean to ask the question "how do we know what we know about the pain and anguish of the racial divide in America? Why can't we listen, see, feel, and affirm the humanity of the other? How do we better understand the wounds created by patterns of systemic racism? All of us did not voluntarily come over to America gazing at the "Statue of Liberty," which evoked dreams of opportunity and success in the new land.

But others came as captives as in the belly of slave ships, as far back as 1619. This too, is a vital piece of the American Story that must be accepted, affirmed, and ethically internalized—in order to bring true healing and hope to broken communities among us, "from sea to shining sea!"

For ordinary folk of goodwill and ethically sensitive persons, we cannot honestly—go on to fully understand the blessings of liberty and opportunity in America, without grappling with the agonizing burden of racial bigotry, often couched in the rituals of denial and the mystic pretensions of living in a color-blind society.

Now some American writers and social critics seem to distinguish between at least three dominant types of racism. These may include: a) individual racism; b) institutional racism; and c) cultural racism. Race, per se, is a complex socio-historical concept. It is not easily defined. Some elements may include "belief in racial superiority and inferiority;" strong in-group preference, as well as the rejections of outsiders. Still other social critics may see racism as a wild weed growing in the garden of humanity.

Accordingly, the insightful volume, *Prejudice and Racism*, by James M. Jones sees "individual racism" as a form of thinking closely aligned with race prejudice itself. Historically, Jones goes on to quote Abraham Lincoln, as expressive of individual racist thinking: *"I am not, nor ever have been, in favor of bringing about in any way the social and political equality of the white and black races."*[7]

Now a second type of racism may be described as "institutional racism." This particular type appeared to be far more entrenched

---

7. Jones, Prejudice and Race, 13.

into the corporate patterns of our common life. For example, the Riot Commission (also known as the *Kerner Report*), goes beyond the level of individual racism to a more insidious form, with a biting edge, that concluded, in part, that "America is moving toward two societies: one white and one black—separate and unequal." I suspect that this report, which grew out of the turbulent years of the 1960s—bears a strange relevance to the perennial racial unrest in the Ferguson Movement today. A third type of expression cited by James M. Jones is "cultural racism." Generally, he cites cultural racism as an in-group belief, clinging impulse that holds the "superiority of one cultural heritage over that of another race."[8] Here it seems to me that people who are marginalized, undervalued, systemically powerless have a greater chance of "feeling" locked out of opportunities in pursuit of the American Dream. I don't know, but I suspect, that these "feelings" of being locked-out, feelings of inequality by the law, and "feelings" of police use of excessive force are close to the heart, systemically, of the Ferguson Movement. The ethical implications here are enormous for all who love peace, justice, and the rebuilding community.

On the one hand, the dashing waves of "Lament and Hope" are dynamic and interdependent as we continue to explore the long shadow of the Ferguson Movement in the real search for peace and justice, understanding and accountability, and the stubbornness of faith to rebuild a broken community. On the other hand, I think that the "lament" involves the courage to comeback—economically and commercially __ from the hot ashes of the fire, saying:

"*We will not be defeated by the unexpected storm . . . that blew against our city!*" After all, as one old Ferguson resident quipped: "*Only those who have been tried in the fire, will not scorch in the sun!*" Moreover, the language of the "lament" points toward a variety of meanings, including that which is "sorrowful," "grievous," "terrible," "dreadful," "hurtful," "painful," and "exceedingly unfortunate"—being caught in the grips of loss and personal destruction. It seems to me that what is really at stake is the capacity for us to recognize these residual factors of lamentation. The language

---

8. Ibid., 14

of "hope" involves the courage-to-be. Undoubtedly, the courage-to-be itself involved nothing less than a wave of peaceful voices speaking out for justice. We shall further take a closer look at the waves and dynamics of the "lament"—socially and ethically. I am the first to admit that the "lament," self-examination and prayer itself (1Thes 5:17), is difficult and challenging for us all. Critically speaking, we will start first with the lament, because it is ever before us.

Now the *American College Dictionary* defines, functionally speaking, the "lament" as the moment or place to "feel and express sorrow." For the human community, it involved empathy to express "mourning and grief." Being etymologically derivative from the Latin word, *lamentari*, meaning "absence" or "loss."[9] As I see it, through the lens of my own experience and observations—so many people of rationality and compassionated goodwill deeply lamented the absence of Michael Brown, Jr. from human community, from the ordinary friendships and rites of passage to chase one's dream.

Michael Brown, Jr., I lament, because you represent anybody's son in Ferguson or elsewhere—caught in a web of tragic, disruptive, and unlawful circumstances that violated the sensibility of law enforcement. Contrary to the expressed opinion of some folk, he was not—as one counter-protestor shouted, *"just another thug who got what he deserved!"* Perhaps, the language of reason and hope tell a different story; and challenge the best-in-us to consider an alternative narrative. A narrative laced with voices of two brothers. One is irony; the second one is hope. Metaphorically, the narrative is anchored in two sisters. One is justice baptized in love. The second sister is mutual understanding baptized in compassionate reforms in police-community relationships, as the necessary bridge to rebuilding and establishing vehicles of trust.

Here, when I use the word diary, three functional clues and conceptual understandings come to mind. In the first place, my conceptual understanding of the term "diary" itself involved an attempt to achieve a broader view of the Ferguson Movement. Here

9. Barnhart, ed., American College Dictionary, 684.

I mean to suggest that the notion of "diary" is a literary expression, in search of the truth as seen through the eyes of the observer—as experienced in a given location. For example, this conceptual location can be, undoubtedly, observed and experienced almost anywhere. Now, my own journey or conceptual location is St. Louis County—and nearby Ferguson, in particular, where I have shopped, dined, had my car serviced, worshipped, and found expressions of friendship and hospitality for many years in the city of Ferguson. In the second place, I have attempted to use the word "diary" to talk about the themes of "lament" and "hope" and how we move forward. As such, diary always aims at a true and honest accounting of real experiences and facts—whether it falls in the conceptual categories of protestors or counter-protestors, as seen from different perspectives, and alterative angles of vision. To be sure, I recognize that my "angle of vision"—deeply—reflects my social background, culture, and religious upbringing as an African American father, husband, Christian ethicist, author, pastor, poet, and little league soccer coach in St. Louis County.

In the third place, I suspect that the functional use of the word "diary" aims at the desire for impartiality and fairness, responsibility and mutual efforts to build bridges of trust and cooperation between police officers and the communities they serve, and young teens of color in particular.

The critical moments of reason, in any case, and search for common ground—must prevail in order to make better communities of goodwill in conflicted neighborhoods. Therefore, *the lighthouse of "hope" is a wave upon the ocean of life.* Facing the twin realities of "lament" and "hope," I suspect that we can only move forward as we turn—compassionately and intelligently—to each other, rather than on each other. Perhaps, in this last section of our observations, entitled "Lament and Hope," we may begin to crack open new horizons of understanding to positively move forward.

Hope is such an important value in our common humanity. When we get up each morning, we consciously or subconsciously **_hope_** that all will go well in the course of the day. If we are working, we **_hope_** for a stress-free work environment in the market place. If we are not formally working, we **_hope_** to find a job. If we have children or grand-children, loved-ones or parents—we certainly **_hope_** for Divine favor and earthly blessings! Honestly, can you think of any social situation—either in the Ferguson unrest or elsewhere—in life that you don't **_hope_** for something?

Without a doubt, the key question in this moment of self-reflection—is simply this: *"What is worth hoping for?"*

For example, the good book teaches us that our hope is tied-in with our faith (Heb 11.1). Our faith is tied-in with our <u>character</u>. An expression of this notion is found in 1 Timothy 4:12, which says: *". . . be thou an example of the believers, in work, in conversation, in charity, in spirit, in faith, in purity."*

First, we may discover—surprisingly as humans—that the making of character is a gift that we receive from the Divine. "If we have God in all things while they are ours, says Cicero," we shall have all things in God when they are taken away."[10] Certainly, we can see evidence of this hope and shining character in the personality of the African American patriotic hero: Crispus Attucks.

Secondly, the providential thing that Crispus Attucks hoped for was independence for all Americans from the oppressive rule of British "red coats." From the viewpoint of America's deep story, Crispus Attucks was the first human being to give his life in battle for American Independence.[11] Of course, history tells us that he was an ex-runnerway slave from Framingham, MA who had fled from his so called "master" (i.e., William Brown), two decades earlier. Equipped with character, courage, and hope—this patriotic battle took place on Monday, March 5, 1770.[12]

Thirdly, we as humans can be assured that the Divine Force is always in our battle for **hope** and **independence**! Finally, brothers and sisters, the Divine Force wants us to have an independent spirit. But what—after all—is independence? Here I think that it can be defined as <u>self-motivation</u> to <u>find</u> our <u>own way</u>, to be <u>creative</u>, and to <u>trust God</u> to realize our own <u>potential</u>.

10. Cicero, New Dictionary of Thoughts, 235
11 Toppin, Blacks in America, 48
12. Ibid., 49–50.

Coming full circle in Ferguson, we hope for an environment in the market place, where our children can experience the fruits of laughter, love, play, safety, peace, and educational excellence. They are our hope. They are the nudging elbows that closely cuddle to us at night—locked into the security of family, love and nurture. They are symbolic of our own DNA and legacy.

Personally, I am reminded of hope not despair when I think about the people living in the communities of Ferguson—whose souls have been tried in the fire of loss, disappointments, violence, anger, and perplexity. Yet, the craving of the human spirit is to bounce back! Here the Bible clearly replies, I believe, with a shining ray of hope—whether we are children or adults. It says:

> "... *we have this treasure in clay jars, so that it may be made clear that this extraordinary power belongs to God and does not come from us. We are afflicted in every way, but not crushed; perplexed, but not driven to despair; persecuted, but not forsaken; struck down, but not destroyed."*
>
> —(2Cor 4:7–9 NRSV)

To be sure, the redemptive word of the gospel is—for many persons of color in particular—our historical heritage; but it is the hope in knowing that our children are our future! Biblically, little children are special, as the power of God is extraordinary. Be that as it may—for protestors and residents alike—our children are the main reason we can "chant" or carry a sign reading, **"I love Ferguson!" "We Love Ferguson!"** Our children—like the promising landscape of other municipalities—live, move, and have their being in Ferguson. Our children of America—and all those who work for rebuilding mutual responsibility and understanding, peace, and the drum beat of justice—is our future.

Now in terms of future reform and development, I suspect, as a concerned St. Louis County resident, the following possibilities appear to be in order. **First**, the importance of continuing the positive economic, economic, educational, inter-racial, religious, and geopolitical initiatives that are already underway. **Secondly**, the indispensability of a viable vehicle for the improvement of police-community relations.

For example, in some areas of our nation, this may take the form of establishing a functional Civilian Review Board. **Thirdly**, God's love requires justice and respect for all persons: red, yellow, black or white, we are all equally precious in God's sight. **Fourth**, Genetically, people are not born with racism; rather it is acquired through certain social habits and attitudes in our family life and culture. **Fifth**, churches and concerned people must confront the dominant white media in our culture to eliminate residual negative stereotypes of African Americans, Latinos, Asians, Native Americans, the disabled and abused, gays and lesbians, the mentally and physically challenged, and other victims of mistreatment. **Sixth**, Despite the gains of the civil rights movement in the '60s and its vision of an integrated society, the "symbolic 11 o'clock hour of worship" on Sunday is, perhaps, still the most segregated hour in American life.[13] **Seventh**, The moral imperative is this: Don't keep silent![14] Americans have an obligation to struggle against all forms of bigotry and abuse.

As a father, I suspect that the generation that stirs our passion the most is the generation of our children. We seem to want a world free of violence, terrorism, repression, injustice, and the fear that robs our children of their innocence and capacity to dream. In our children, we see ourselves. We see our gleaming hope for tomorrow. Flawed and imperfect as we all are, children today have more need of positive role-models than negative folk—who often deny racial bigotry.

Yet the lingering thread of hope, reflected in the voices and rhythms of our children, is still enmeshed in the pain and suffering of the racial divide in America. This critical issue is in the heart of ordinary folk; it begs the attention not to be—either ignored

---

13. Oglesby, Living at the Intersection of Race and Religion, 16.
14. Ibid., 16.

or denied by some—swepted under a rug again. Hope cannot live without the "rug"—symbolically—being recognized and dismantled. Hope is a chorus that we learn to sing <u>together</u>, or the thieves of history will take away the melodious lyrics. Given the waves of "Lament and Hope," we shall now unpack some of the "sayings," peculiar to my own observations, reflections and experiences:

1. A drive-by shooting, I lament, is a crocked stick; but people of goodwill must hit a straight lick with a crooked-stick.

2. Police brutality—in or out of uniform—is a crooked stick; but ordinary people of goodwill must hit a straight lick with a crooked-stick.

3. I lament reckless violence of any-kind, because violence for the sake of violence leads only to more violence.

4. The impulse of racial mis-trust, I lament, is a crooked stick; but the God of universe empowers us to hit a straight lick with a crooked-stick.

5. Bigotry of any kind is a crooked stick; but ordinary people can hit a straight lick with a crooked-stick.

6. Peace divorced from justice is a crooked stick; yet young leaders of the Ferguson movement challenge us to hit a straight lick with a crooked-stick.

7. Big efforts of touch love in rebuilding the Ferguson community are on-going—symbolic of urban centers of revitalization around the nation.

8. Agonizing voices of our youth speak clearer than our eyes are willing to see.

9. Hitting a straight lick with a crooked stick begs the lingering question: "*Why can't we listen to each other, and not turn on each other?*"

10. Hitting a straight lick with a crooked stick begs the lament: "*Why can't I see or imagine Michael Brown, Jr.—flawed, imperfect, as we all are—as my own son who wrongfully took a hand full of cigars from a local store in Ferguson?*"

11. Was this act committed by an 18 year old teenager of the neighborhood right?
12. "Of course not!" But if the 18 year old teenager had been white—doing the same thing from the neighborhood, would the tragic consequences be the same?
13. In the long struggle for social justice, what won't make us bitter will make us better!
14. Hitting a straight lick with a crooked stick begs the "lament," can I really be at peace with myself, when the sounds for justice still ring loud deep in my soul?
15. The sweet echoes of peace and the drum beats of justice must meet one another on the street of "one-accord" in Ferguson and elsewhere.
16. Hitting a straight lick with a crooked-stick emphatically says: *"Body cameras for our police officers who protect us, are not optional but must be required."*
17. O Lord, you are able to transform our communal brokenness and pain in Ferguson; and turn it into a blessing (Ps147:1–3; Rom12:2).
18. O Lord, thank you, that you have created from one blood all the people on Planet Earth (Gen1:1, Ps105:1–2).
19. God's humanity is universal. There is no black humanity; there is no white humanity. There is only one humanity.
20. Hitting a straight lick with a crooked stick sees the love of justice as a transformer of relations between police officers and our teens—regardless of the color line.
21. Justice floats upon a sea of ethics; or it can't float at all.
22. The **hope** of justice means giving to each child—8 years old or 18 years old—his/her due.
23. Peace protestors in the Ferguson movement or beyond seem to discern the tender balance between "speaking the truth to power," and "speaking the truth in love."

24. As a Christian believer, I lament the actions of any individual, who fails to take seriously this tender balance into account.

25. I observed some voices from Ferguson's street corner crowd lamentably shout, "what if Michael Brown, Jr. had been your own child?"

26. Where are the strong grass-roots vehicles of dialogue, I lament, that lead to common ground?

27. Where are the strong grass-roots vehicles, I lament, that may give birth to rebuilding, and the healing of the wounded spirit in America?

28. Am I not responsible for my own energy and intelligence to reach out and help rebuild broken relationships in community?

29. If not me, who? If not now, when?

30. Let every child—black or white—write his or her own narrative, rather than being chained by the mis-perceptions of others!

31. Agents of **Hope** estranged in the endless battles of life know that every break-down can lead to a break-through.

32. Agents of **Hope** anticipate and suspect that Ferguson's trials and tribulations—or in other cities—are only clouds of darkness before the crack of dawn.

33. Waves and voices from the Ferguson movement seem to shout, "Never mind the strange faces behind the mask; our main goal is staying focus on the task!"

34. Except for shouts of a justice-filled peace, why bother about raising a big-fuss, God has already promised to be with us (Mt 28:19–20).

35. As human agents of **Hope**, I suspect that the Holy One has an extraordinary sense of humor.

36. **Hope** anticipates and restores.

37. We all are—as agents of hope—beautifully flawed (Rom 3:23).
38. Agents of **hope**, I suspect, reject the seductive path of drugs, drinking, and drifting—peculiar to some teens and adults alike.
39. Agents of **hope**, deeply believe that "safety-to-all" is the "Big Deal," an unifying thread for both police officers and the general public.
40. For Ferguson, I suspect, the only viable option for rebuilding, is rebuilding.
41. Chaos and senseless violence are not viable options in a civil society.
42. Yet, I lament, in 2014 St. Louis' 159 homicides, how, then, do we say: *"Let respect for basic humanity abide?"*
43. Where is God, I lament, when senseless violence for some, seem to overshadow the love of non-violence for all?
44. I lament, O God, the silence and absence of the Michael Browns of society; but I wonder *"Why do some folk seem to be demonized and called street-thugs?"*
45. I lament, O God, why can't we attempt to feel the other's pain, and seek to understand the other's journey?
46. **Hope** is fanning the flames of expectation.
47. Every forward movement to build bridges of trust is **hope**.
48. **Hope** is not rooted in phony love, false promises, and formal citations by public officials.
49. Many American Christians are too drunk on love-talk and too silent on justice-walk (Amos 5:21–24).
50. In the rhythmic flux of hope, you gotta go from Mr. Dude to Ms. Lucky in rebuilding the neighborhoods.
51. In the rhythmic flux of hope, be aware that the same people who may "praise" you in the morning," may "crucify" you in the evening!

52. What keeps us together, as moral activists anchored in **hope**, is compassion for others; and reliance upon a God who brought us through great suffering in the wilderness (Ex 20:1–2).

53. We are a nation steeped in the values of freedom and **hope**, fully grounded in the iconic Latin phrase, *e pluribus enum* (i.e., "out of many, one").

54. **Hope** is the courage to believe—given the Fergusons around the world—in the unseen hand of God to transform and restore broken lives (Rom 12:1–2).

55. **Hope** is the power to say: "We're still standing!"

56. **Hope** is the capacity to believe— especially in the hearts of the poor and down-trodden—that the gospel scratches, where we itch (Lk 4:18–19).

57. Did I ever tell you that forgiveness of others is healing for your own soul? (2Chron 7:14; Matt 18:21–22).

58. Unchain our hands, O Lord, to work for peace; unchain our feet to run for justice.

59. Unchain our ears, O Lord, so we can hear, again, the tender voices of children cry out: "Let's build a world of peace and kindness that begins with ME, ME, ME!" (Matt 18:3).

60. **Hope** is the garment of confident expectation as I shop and walk the streets of Ferguson, or wherever I may live.

61. **Hope** is the pot-liquor of collard greens, long after the aroma of collard greens are gone!

62. Let the force of **hope** rise-up from the landscape of the poor and marginalized, to the rich and privileged ones in our social order (Matt 19:24).

63. **Hope** speaks truth to power.

64. Funky rhythms of despair are no match for the dawn of sunshine—inspiring inner strength (Is 40:29–31).

65. Yet, hope cries aloud in the streets of Ferguson: "We Need Our Jobs!"

66. Some folk believe that we have taken three steps forward in black-white relations and five steps backward: but the unending imperative is this:

    "KEEP ON STEPPING!"

67. **Hope** is the rhythms of shout, dance and praise to the Almighty (Ps 150:1–6).

68. **Hope** is self-acceptance in the awareness of a God who made us the way we are: that is a beautiful thing!

69. (Ps 100:1–5).

70. **Hope** is the quiet assurance to believe that "what-is," can be changed to "what ought-to-be."

71. **Hope** builds bridges to invite ordinary folk in; rather than walls to keep ordinary people out.

5

Case Studies

> Education is an ocean;
> And every child born in the universe
> Has the right to sail that ocean.
>
> —African Proverb

Introduction

On the one hand, the extraordinary strokes of the democratic election of 2008—affirming Barack Obama as the first black president of the United States of America—set off a tidal wave of hope. It was joyfully marked by many American citizens as a "revolution of rising expectations."[1] On the other hand, it was a reactionary period—for some folk—in our collective social life marred by white backlash, racial fear, and that demonic flame of visible and invisible racism.[2]

Indeed, a mixed bag of emotions, fears, suspicions that make it difficult for us to honestly talk about the lingering "white

---

1. Oglesby, Convocation Breakfast, Eden Seminary, St. Louis, MO, 2009.
2. Ibid., 2009.

elephant" in the living room as we fast forward to the promise of 2015—in terms of opportunity and hope for a better tomorrow.

Thus the practical inclusion of case studies in this small book, fictionalized as they are, may crack open a deeper level of understanding about actual problems and circumstances some people struggle with living in Ferguson as well as in cross-cultural communities elsewhere in our great nation. Be that as it may, the primary function of a case is to lift-up a chunk of reality, for the purpose of genuine dialogue, new vistas of learning, self-understanding, spiritual growth and change.[3] Now, we go into these cases and see what their possibilities and ethical implications are for all of us seeking justice and hope in the Ferguson community, and elsewhere in our land.[4]

Case 1: Concession Stand Moms

Mary Anne is a 40 year old single parent of three children. She is an African American mom, who volunteered to serve behind the concession stand for the general public. Her daughter, Ashantee is 14 years old, and a very good team player in baseball, at a magnet school in the city of St. Louis. On the one hand, Ashantee and her mother Mary Anne are what social critics call "North-siders" in St Louis County—being predominantly black. On the other hand, Linda, who is 38 years old, is the mother of two daughters, Susan, 15, who is a baseball team mate of Ashantee. Both Linda and her daughter Susan are Caucasian. Given the historic patterns of racial division (i.e. *de facto* balkanization*)*, blacks and whites never had—seemingly—a mutually viable chance to interact with each other as human beings. Thus Linda and Susan are what some locals call "South-siders."

Unintentionally, concession stands can be impartial to real surprises: gleaming eyes that see each other for the first time, hands that volunteer to serve hot dogs and soft drinks for the first

---

3. Oglesby, Born In The Fire, 11–12.
4. Ibid., 10.

time, and smiles that meet for the first time, discovering, enthusiastically, that their own children are supportive competitors on the same middle school baseball team. The lingering question that haunts me still, "can Mary Anne and Linda take this unexpected encounter to a higher level of mutual regard and understanding as Concession Stand Moms?

In the rhythmic flux of time, I learned several weeks later that Mary Anne and Linda had decided to get together for fellowship with their children to attend a St. Louis Cardinal Baseball game. To be sure, "Moms"—for the most part—are nurturing mothers. One old saying that joyfully flooded my spirit as logged in my diary was this: *"God couldn't be everywhere, so God created mothers!"* Well, it is at least something to chew on as ordinary folk in human community. Surprisingly, why not have more moms or dads to volunteer at concession stands?

Case 2: Rapping Cops!

"We both have the same interest in saving young teenagers from the rough streets . . . because many of them live right here on our beat — on the West Side." These are the words from Ralph Middleton, an African American police officer, 36 years old, who has served on the Detroit Police Force for the past ten years. These words were spoken to Harold Davis, a Caucasian, 34 years old, assigned to the same beat for one year.

After several months in the trenches of survival, they became close friends. Ralph was a former "rapper" in the neighborhood and knew the "ins and outs" of inner city life.

Accordingly, Harold began to hang out with Ralph; and slowly Harold became amazed by the powerful rhythmic lyrics of Rap Music. All along, Ralph taught his friend some of the basic expressions of hip-hop culture and "Rap" in the city. Meanwhile, they both begin to brainstorm one evening—during Happy Hour, and after a few beers—about the possibility of "rap" as a tool to "breaking-the-ice" and gradually winning trust with young teenagers, living on their beat, off of Chicago Blvd and Lynnwood Ave.,

Case Studies

and on the West Side of Detroit. Now Malik Campbell, 15 years old, is a troubled and rebellious teenager who lives with his mother of two other siblings—Alice, 12 years old, and an older brother Larry, who was 17 years of age before he became a tragic victim of a drive-by shooting of Lynnwood Ave. on the West Side of Detroit.

After facing waves of danger everyday to safeguard the public good, Ralph posed certain questions to Harold, "Why don't we try to use 'Rap' to reach some teenagers in the city?" "What can we really lose?" "Teens can't feel anymore disconnected and angry—some at us—than they do right now in our society? Where is mutual accountability?" While loving their professional work, Ralph and Harold came up with two goals around the sideline venture of "rapping" with teens, "Let's try and keep kids off the streets packing guns,"—says Ralph to Harold. This was their first goal. Ralph further quipped to his friend: "Let's keep them on the school yard, rather than in the graveyard." This was their second goal. For a few months, police officer Davis and police officer Middleton confronted young Malik with the question: "Malik, do you really know what it is like for a black teenager to grow up in America and find success without education or careful guidance from the ruthless violence of the streets?" In any event, it is in dealing with dudes like you that finally some troubled teens—on the streets of Detroit—begin to respect and see us as the "Rapping Cops!"

Case 3: Caught-in-the-Wilderness

"What's the use of going on?" I work hard all the time, as a proud resident in Ferguson. Sadly, "my efforts at hard work,"—Samuel angrily complained, "All went up in smoke last night . . . in looting, stealing, and taking." "Like an unexpected blast from hell, I once had a thriving business here in Ferguson," says Samuel, "but now I see nothing but ashes."

However, the flipside of the reckless economic loss of property is the rising tide of racial division between black and white residents in Ferguson. For example, back in August, 2014, after the Michael Brown's shooting—a survey suggested that 80% of

African Americans viewed the matter as having important racial overtones, whereas only 44% of whites felt the same way.[5] In a comparative chart on achievements by race and class, states the fact that Ferguson's police force is 7% black, while its general population is over—approximately—21,000 is 67% black.

Respectfully, the St. Louis County police force is 10% black, while the population of St. Louis County is 24% black. Referred to by some sociologists as the "new urban underclass," the St. Louis City police force is 34% black, whereas the population of St. Louis City is 48% black.[6] Economically, the median income by race in Ferguson reflects a scale of analysis, which places the average black resident with an annual income of approximately $30,000.00, and one's white counter-part at an average annual income rate of slightly under $56,000.00. By any normative standard, race is a slippery slope in America. It cannot be easily affirmed or dismissed as a simple case of white supremacy over ruthless black-rage—taking the forms of riots, burnings, and lootings. But Samuel's business was burned to the ground. He cried out in despair, "Why me, O Lord?" Samuel Peterson is a 40 year old entrepreneur, with a wife, Sarah, 36 and two children, Thomas, 12, and Jennifer, 9 years old. "How did my American Dream come crashing down?"

Case 4: "Lay Down Yo' Burdens!"

In the throws of struggle, anger, pain, fear, mis-trust, and suspicion between certain police officers and certain teenagers—there is a silver lining not in some "Pie-in-the-Sky" theology; but rather in the comforting words born in funky rhythms of what some folks call: "The Ole Negro Spirituals."

Larry a 65 year old retired railroad engineer, recently told his life-long friend, Walter, who is 64 years old, the following uneasy moments—and for some embarrassing stains attached to the lofty ideals of American history. Walter, then, muttered: "wasn't the

---

5. "Race and Class," St. Louis Black and White, 73–74.
6. Ibid., 80–81.

Case Studies

song, '*Lay Down Yo' Burdens*, originally an old work chant used by slaves to help other slaves survive the hard work and painful whip lashes of each day? Walter continues to probe with his friend, Larry, by saying, "Why do we still call this reality only Black History—in the shortest but conspicuous month of February?" "Is not Black History also American History," says Walter, "among us all?" Larry finally admits to Walter, "Maybe some of us can see as residents of Ferguson, a thin redemptive silver lining boldly shouting to all who dare to listen: *'Lay Down Yo" Burdens*!

Case 5: "NO Escape!"

"Honey, I can't sleep this night, let us get up and go right now!" These were the words that dropped from the lips of Smokey, a 38 year old father who lives on the edge of Ferguson, Missouri. Smokey is happily married to Mary, who is 37 years old. They are the proud parents of Wanda, 7 years of age, and little Eric, 5 years old.

The turbulent situation that Smokey is "morally nervous" about in this case, grew out of the critical and nail-biting event of the release of the Grand Jury Decision, regarding police officer Darren Wilson, in the shooting and killing of Michael Brown, Jr. an eighteen year old person. Be that as it may, the Grand Jury reached its long awaited decision a few days before Thanksgiving, Nov. 24, 2014—as the nation and news media outlets around the world looked on in anxious anticipation. When the Grand Jury's curtain was finally raised and etching ears fully opened, the pronouncement of the decision found Darren Wilson released from all alleged charges. Moreover, it was common knowledge, in the hard core the trenches of Ferguson community that the Grand Jury—as reported—was made up of 9 white jurors and only 3 black jurors.

Suddenly, parts of the city of Ferguson and beyond its borders into other municipalities literally exploded in violence, burnings, looting, pain, and moral outrage over what had come to pass. Meanwhile, Smokey made it crystal clear to Mary, his wife of 10 years, — "Honey, I can't sleep, this night, let us get up and go right now!" So then, the "right now" declaration by Smokey involved a change in their Thanksgiving Holiday driving schedule—from St. Louis to Detroit.

In reality, Smokey and his entire family had originally planned on their journey—to leave St. Louis County approximately 6 a.m. a few days before the Thanksgiving festivities. Instead, they left 5 hours earlier, deep into the night. Strangely and ironically, as they packed their car and rolled down interstate I-70 E to Indianapolis, picking up route 69 N. to Fort Wayne, then to 94 E, en route to Detroit—all of the early morning talk radio shows re-vibrated with one concurrent theme: The explosive waves of protest and reckless burnings in Ferguson, Missouri. "Then sounds of the radio helped to keep me awake," said Smokey, "on this tiring trip of 10 hours."

In any event, Smokey retorted to his wife Mary, in an uneasy tone, upon his arrival in the motor city: "Honey, there is no escape!" Being in the trenches of disbelief and anxiety, Smokey and his wife Mary—in particular—found in Detroit what they had just left behind in St. Louis: Protest! Now, both Mary and Smokey found this wave of protest amazingly ironic. As an ethically sensitive person, "What do you think?"

Case 6: Divided We Stand

To paraphrase Lesley McSpadden, who spoke on January 19, 2015 at a celebrative event in St. Louis, Missouri honoring the contributions and social activism of Rev. Dr. Martin Luther King, Jr.—the resounding echo for justice was now! To an ideologically divided audience at Harris Stowe University—the place where the King celebration was held—she seems to say, "don't hit me with two bad attitudes of disrespect . . . one for young Michael, my son, the other for Dr. King . . .. No one has lost more than me . . . pain and all, in this Ferguson unrest."

The real current "Divided We Stand" problematic appears to have many faces and tensions in the community. For instance, Steve Jacobs is a 77 year old civil right activist, who marched with the Martin Luther King Freedom Movement of the early 1960s in their bid for the desegregation of public education. By contrast young Alice Pitmann is a pre-med student at Washington University of St. Louis is an active peace protestor in the Ferguson movement over the last five months. Politically, she is at odds with what she calls the "old timers of the 1960s."

"They are simply out of touch . . . not on the same page with our struggle . . . our history is our own history," says Alice. Another real issue in the "Divided We Stand" dilemma is the conflict between some aggressive protestors and loyal students at Harris–Stowe University. Apparently, certain students felt a need to protect their academic turf—as a load of peace protesters took over and disrupted the regular program to honor the legacy of Martin Luther King, Jr. Again the back drop of political polarization and tension in the air, this was St. Louis' 46th Annual Civic Ceremony to remember and honor the life of Dr. King. Though many leaders, on January 19th, 2015, spoke from the same platform, I observed that the St. Louis community appeared to more divided, antsier, and less unified. There is, apparently, division in the ranks of the struggle for justice, as to what direction to go. For instance, many people observed, who attended the annual ceremony this year (January 19th, 2015, at Harris-Stowe University St. Louis Missouri), that a few fights broke out between regular street protesters and a few college students at Harris-Stowe. One bystander was, then, prompted to say, ". . . how sad, now we got the black-on-black tussle . . . where blacks are turning on each other rather than to each other!"

Ironically, "Divided We Stand." However, the hard question that grips the front burner of our consciousness is simple as it is awesome, namely: Is there a basic disconnect between young protestors of the Ferguson movement and older community activists, who marched with Dr. King and others in the cause for justice?

Case 7: "Is There a Generational Gap?"

Our struggle is not white on black, it's not between the powerful over against the powerless, "says Al—a young African American peace protestor—"rather it is the growing tension in the way we approach social justice in 2014, as junior achievers, as over against what you guys did for "civil right" in the 1960s as senior achiever. In terms of background, Al is an ethically sensitive person, who majored in psychology at Washington University, located in St. Louis, Missouri. Al is an intellectually gifted, student, who is well respected by his peers in campus and community affairs.

Al appears to be a natural born leader. He is 21 years old, and a senior student on track, academically, for graduation in a year or so. Regarding the perceived tension and inward weary, Al shared this concern about the generational-gap with Rebecca, who is 20 years old and a pre-med student at Washington University. "Some of us who are out there in the streets today, marching for justice in the case of Michael Brown, Rebecca finds it hard to connect with what people did way back in that era." With a puzzled look on her face, she muttered "I don't really feel comfortable with a lot of old folks trying to tell me what to do—and what strategies to use." She continues by positively shouting, "Ferguson is our movement, Al, this is our time!" Is the so called generation-gap real between young folk and the elders in the community? Can we really connect, or do we really want to connect?

Case 8: "Charles, I never heard of Kwanzaa?"

Charles is now 17 years old. He is a devout young Black Muslim, living in the province of North St. Louis County. Kevin is a 16 year old African American Christian, who lives with his mother, Muoeshi, a single parent who works to provide for her three children—with Charles being the oldest of the siblings. Economically, the mother, Muoeshi, works full-time at a local Wal-Mart Store, but the money is barely enough for family survival.

Meanwhile, Kevin—Charles closest friend has become deeply curious about the cultural celebration of Kwanzaa, which is now recognized around the traditional Advent Season. But what, then, is Kwanzaa? Well, the cultural celebration of Kwanzaa itself is the creation of Professor Maulana Karenga, cited in his book

Case Studies

Kwanzaa: A celebration of family and community and culture, which describes how certain organic fruits harvest come together in the bosom of ordinary folk—around the cultural symbols of food, music, drums, and dance. "Well and good," said Kevin, "but Charles what is Kwanzaa really all about?" I'm still confused and cannot make a connection to the Ferguson unrest?" Historically, creator of Kwanzaa, in the ethical thought of Professor Karenga, was designed to be a communal word—just like the symbolic shout, "We Love Ferguson!" Organically, the notion of Kwanzaa is related to seven key values, called Nguzo Saba[7] (that is to say, the Seven Principles, which included the following: Unity, Self-Determination, Collective Work and Responsibility, Cooperative Economics, Purpose, Creativity, and Faith).[8] For example, Kevin forthrightly asked Charles these amazing questions: *Will these principles help restore and rebuild the brokenness and hurt of Ferguson? What are the relational principles that I may get my head and heart around?*

Case 9: "Praise God outside the Box!"

Jeremiah and Jack are Christians and longtime resident of the city of Ferguson, Missouri. Jeremiah is a 37 year old African American male, who worked hard to successfully achieve a university degree in electrical engineering. He is currently full-time employed at Emerson Electric Company in Ferguson. Jeremiah is a proud father and husband to Delores, 35 years old. They are happily married, with a beautiful daughter, Michelle, who is 7 years old.

Jack is a 36 year old Caucasian, who so happens to work at Emerson Electric as an electrical engineer. In terms of occupational status, Jack has been with the company for three years—experiencing, like Jeremiah, promotional success up the corporate ladder. Jack is still single, but committed to a serious relationship. By pure coincidence, Jack and Jeremiah got acquainted one day in

---

7. Karenga, Kwanzaa, 43–44.
8. Ibid., 45–66.

the lunchroom. Thereafter, they saw each other, causally, several times during the lunch break. Gradually, Jack begins to open up and told Jeremiah that he had a drinking problem; but it didn't seem to affect his job performance as an engineer. Jack, then, started to feel more comfortable in sharing this secretive experience with Jeremiah to the point where the actual sharing made a positive difference. As Christians, both love the church and its service in the community. Yet both men were shocked, bewildered, and morally disturbed over the shooting of Michael Brown, Jr. by police officer Darren Wilson, August 9th, 2014. The immediate waves of tumultuous unrest kept vibrating around the nation and our fragile global village. Meanwhile, Jeremiah and Jack wondered as Christians, "what would it be like if we worshipped God in different places?" Or "may be at your church," says Jeremiah. "May be at your place of worship," retorted Jack? Did you know, explained Jeremiah "that the most segregated hour of the week, allegedly, is Sunday morning worship?"

Perhaps this is true with deep established ethnic traditions of cliquishness in parts of St. Louis. But Jeremiah made a bold move toward Jack in saying, "Man praise God outside the box —- come and go to worship with me this forthcoming Sunday morning." *"To think outside—the box,"* quipped Jeremiah *"is one thing —- but to praise, shout, and sing to the beats of God's mercy and justice will pull us to a whole new level!"* As Deacon Jones, a longtime church member often says: *"Will you come sing with us, and make the devil a liar?"* (See—Ps 100; Ps 150 cf)

Case 10: When Two Worlds Meet

Young Michael Adams is a 7 year old child, who recently made friends with Jacob Hershell, who is also 7 years old, as both boys are classmates at Cassidy C. Smith Elementary School, in Ferguson, Missouri. Now, after several weeks of basketball playing—in the gym—during recess, Michael invites Jacob for a casual "sleepover" in his home. Michael is white—Jacob is black. Undoubtedly, with the consent of both parents, young Jacob gladly accepts the

Case Studies

invitation! After a satisfying pizza party, Mike replied, "I don't usually visit anyone outside my neighborhood . . . but this is nice." Jacob replied, "I don't either!" "Everyone else I see on T.V." says Jacob, "is upset about different stuff . . . here where we live." Then, young Mike goes on to ask Jacob, "Tell me about your feelings?"

Case 11: "Daddy, Can We Go and See the Big Animals?"

Little Scott Anderson attends the public school system in St. Charles, Missouri. He is in the second grade, at John F. Kennedy Elementary School. Young Scott is 7 years old and athletically gifted in soccer—or so it appears. Not that it matters to kids, but Scott is also Caucasian. Now Scott's best friend in his class is Ben Jenkins, who is 7 years old. Ben is an African American. Physically active, Ben himself loves both soccer and basketball!

Notwithstanding, both Ben and Scott live in the same middle class neighborhood, in St. Charles county—perhaps the most fastest growing county in the whole state of Missouri. Scott's father, David, is a small business owner. He runs a successful Dry Cleaner's Store, on Kingshighway, in downtown St. Charles. David is also a single parent, a father raising a younger child—with love and discipline—outside of the traditional bonds of marriage. In short, David is the father of two children: Scott and Lois. With amazing energy, Lois, the baby is only 2 years old. Ben's father, Henry, is an African American police officer, who has been on the county force for five years, in public service and safety in the community. Both Scott and Ben as friends, attend the same neighborhood local church.

Curiously for some, but very common for many kids, Scott invites Ben to his home for a "sleep-over." Ben gladly accepts the invitation. During the evening, they had fun with games, snacks, and music. But somewhere in the evening, the intriguing Bible verse, *"Suffer little children to come unto me —- of such is the kingdom of heaven"* (Mt.19:14) was the topic of lighthearted conversation among the kids. They ask both young fathers, David and Henry,

"What's up with this special place of little children in the heart of Jesus?" It seems to me—as a father and grandfather myself—that the web of love involves at least four ingredients: a) <u>Permission</u> and encouragement to grow and explore, but also the right of the parent at times to firmly say "YES or NO;" b) <u>Protection</u>, is a seriously precious value in an unforgiving world; c) <u>Possibility</u>, by this I mean the capacity to inspire our children to dream—BIG—for example, who would have imagined in the National Black Community that the day would come when we can behold a black man, living in the White House, as President of the United States of America; in a celebrative mode, an ordinary black preacher in the streets of Washington D.C. shouted aloud: *"There is no secret what God can do!" "Young children keep on dreaming!"* and d) <u>Prayer</u>, by this I mean to suggest the value of teaching our children the simply lesson that prayer is a continuing friendly conversation with God."[9] (1 Thes 5:17)

Finally, the next morning after the sleep-over, Scott enthusiastically asked his father: *"Daddy, can we go and see the Big-Animals at the St. Louis Zoo?"*

> *A white child might need*
> *a role model, but a black child*
> *needs more than that*
> *in this society.*
> *He needs hope.*
>
> —Hank Aaron, Baseball star

---

9. Oglesby, Unpublished original cases.

6

*Study Questions

No one saves us but ourselves
No one can, and no one may;
We ourselves must walk the path,
Teachers merely show the way.

—Black folk proverb

1. What must happen in federal, state, and local governments in order to rebuild the infrastructure of Ferguson, and other cities in need of reform between police departments and communities in which they serve?
2. How can Ferguson serve as a constructive role-model for other cities like Baltimore and Cleveland, in terms of systemic reform in regard to racial profiling, the use of "deadly force," and police retraining to better safeguard all of us?
3. What is the role of community leaders, churches, and institutions of "higher learning" as instruments of healing, justice, and rebuilding?

4. Never forget "Selma's" bloody hallowed grounds, but must we not always remember the human spirit of Michael Brown?

5. How can ordinary people of goodwill use these tragic shootings in cities across our beloved nation as a way to light a candle, rather than to curse the darkness?

6. How can "body-cameras" better enhance public safety, accuracy of events, and the wellbeing and safety of our police officers? (Be specific).

7. Is it not imperative to begin—honestly talking about race—in our own families, homes, churches, communities, schools, and places of work? If not now, when? If not us, who?

8. In respect and honor of Michael Brown, Jr., and all other precious children of God so "wrongfully" victimized, the old folk of the black church used to say: "Every goodbye ain't gone, and every shut eye ain't sleep!" Concretely, how do we make sense out of this saying?

9. What do we teach or say about young or old persons with a different skin-color and social background?

10. As one constructive reform, why not require police officers throughout our nation—black or white—to do field education visits to local Black Museums, followed by conversations on the experience—with the goal of relationship building between officers and people living in the neighborhoods?

11. . Is it true that our neighborhoods won't get any better than we make them?

12. Is it true that one's effort must exceed opportunity for a better tomorrow in America?

13. Sometimes, I hear ordinary folk say "In God we Trust," but the lingering question is "Can God Trust Us?"

14. What ought I to do?

15. What are the merits and demerits of Civilian Review Boards over local police departments?

Study Questions

16. How may we more effectively network with other cities, municipalities, and communities around the nation that are grappling with similar concerns?

17. Is anybody listening to the cries for justice and peace among our children, by their simple examples, in leading us on a better path in building a better America?

18. How can our expression of self-accountability increase the waves and rhythms of justice and hope for tomorrow?

> I am because we are; and
> Because we are,
> Therefore, I am.
> —African proverb

* *The "18 Study Questions" are symbolic of the "18 vital years" that Michael Brown, Jr. lived on Planet Earth; and the steadfast belief that the sun light of justice will rise tomorrow: here there is an interconnectedness of Michael Brown's human spirit, around our vast universe.*

Special Note:

The morally courageous RAMS, in my opinion, who showed symbolic support with Ferguson in protest, on Sunday November 30, 2014, in the Edward Jones Dome were RAMS players: Stedman Bailey, Tavon Austin, Jared Cook, Chris Givens and Kenny Britt, according to the St. Louis American Newspaper (December 4–10, 2014).

Bibliography

Barndt, Joseph R. *Dismantling Racism: The Continuing Challenge to White America*. Minneapolis: Augsburg, 1991.
Barnhart, C.L., and Jess Stein, eds. *The American College Dictionary*. New York: Random House, 1995.
Browns, Ralph E., and Jonathan Edwards, eds. *The New Dictionary of Thoughts*. New York: Standard Book, 1964.
Cooperman, Jeanette. "The Color Line." In *St. Louis Black and White*. St. Louis, MO: stlmag.com (Nov., 2014), 70–73.
Danforth III, John. "Education for All." In *St. Louis Black and White*. St. Louis, MO: stlmag.com (Nov., 2014), 82.
Du Bois, W.E. Burghardt. *The Souls of Black Folk*. New York: Fawcett, 1953.
Hirsch, E. D. Jr., et al., eds. *The Dictionary of Cultural Literacy*. Boston: Houghton Mifflin, 1991.
Jones, James M. *Prejudice and Racism*. New York: The McGraw-Hill Companies, 1997.
Karenga, Maulana. *Kwanzaa: A Celebration of Family, Community, and Culture*. Los Angeles: University of Sankore Press, 1998.
Long, Loren. *Barack Obama of Thee I Sing: A Letter to my Daughters*. New York: Alfred A Knopf, 2010.
Oglesby, Enoch H. *Born in the Fire: Case Studies in Christian Ethics and Globalization*. New York: The Pilgrim, 1990.
———. *Living at the Intersection of Race and Religion*. St. Louis, MO: Eden Theological Seminary, 1995.
———. "Unmasking the Pain." In *Collaboration: A Collection of Poems*. St. Louis, MO: Rycraw, 1991, 65–76.
———. "Unpublished Original Cases: An Ethical Response to the Ferguson Movement." St. Louis, MO: (Spring) 2015.
Oglesby, Joe Nathan. "Courage Brother, God Be With You." In *The Christian Education Conference*, St. James Missionary Baptist Church, Earle, Arkansas, 1962.
Toppin, Edgar A. *A Biographical History of Blacks in America Since 1528*. New York: David McKay Company, 1969.
West, Cornel, and Kevin Shawn Sealey. *Restoring Hope*. Boston: Beacon. 1997.

About the Author

E. Hammond Oglesby, Ph.D

E. Hammond Oglesby, Professor Emeritus, is the United Church Professor of Theology and History at Eden Theological Seminary in St. Louis, MO and an ordained minister in the National Baptist Convention, U.S.A., Inc. He is the author of 11 previous books, including *Pressing Toward the Mark* (2007).

www.ingramcontent.com/pod-product-compliance
Lightning Source LLC
Chambersburg PA
CBHW051702090426
42736CB00013B/2503